CW00970049

Working-Class Life in Victorian Leicester

THE JOSEPH DARE REPORTS

BARRY HAYNES

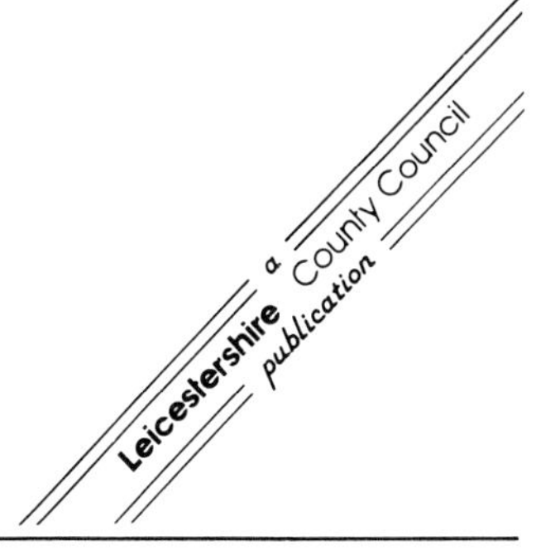

Working-Class Life in Victorian Leicester

THE JOSEPH DARE REPORTS

BARRY HAYNES

Published in 1991 by Leicestershire Libraries and Information Service,
99 Burleys Way, Leicester LE1 3TZ

The publishers would like to thank the following for their kind permission to reproduce photographs and illustrations in their possession.

Information Centre, Bishop Street, Leicester
Museums, Arts and Records Service, New Walk, Leicester
Leicester Mercury, St. Georges Way, Leicester

ISBN 085 022 294X

Designed by Dipak Chauhan
Printed by AB Printers Limited., Leicester

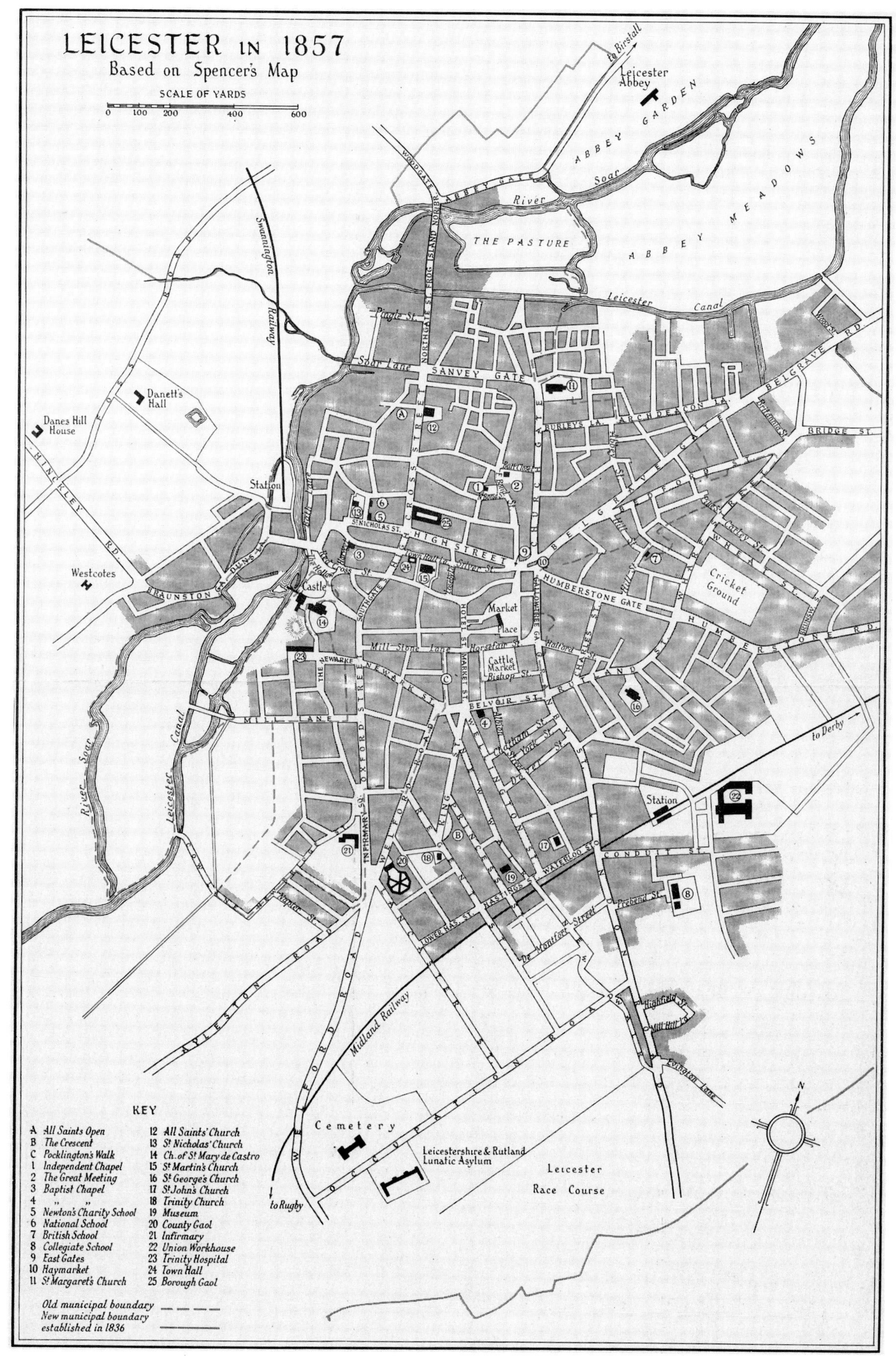

Map of Leicester, 1857

CONTENTS

Leicester looking North from the Cathedral tower c.1860

List of Illustrations

The Clock Tower, 1870s

Introduction

Introduction

The aim of this book is to present an account of working-class life in Victorian Leicester. It is based on the detailed *Annual Reports of the Leicester Domestic Mission*, written by Joseph Dare between 1846-77.

Joseph Dare - Biographical Details[1]

Joseph Dare was born at Titchfield, Hampshire, in 1800. He was one of two pairs of twins in addition to twelve other children. His mother, Hannah Isaacs, was Jewish, whilst his father, Thomas Dare, came from traditional rural stock, his father having been a miller at Bramshott.

The family moved to Hinckley, Leicestershire, whilst Joseph was still young and became attached to the Unitarian congregation there. Only scanty information regarding Joseph's education survives, but it seems probable that it was elementary and received locally. Family tradition speaks of Joseph sacrificing higher learning in order to enable three of his brothers to emigrate to America. Joseph's parents and five of their children joined them in 1841. What is clear, however, is that Joseph loved reading and writing. Throughout his life he wrote poetry, and a book of his verse, *The Garland of Gratitude*, was published in 1849.

In 1830, Joseph married a local girl, Mary Collington. They were to have nine children, though the two eldest daughters both died of fever in 1836. Joseph became a respected member of the Hinckley community as secretary of the Widows and Orphans Society, the Horticultural Society, and other voluntary bodies, in addition to running a boys' school in a room attached to the Unitarian chapel. He also acquired a reputation as an efficient accountant.

In 1845, the Unitarian congregation of the Great Meeting Chapel on East Bond Street, Leicester, was about to establish a Domestic Mission in the town, and required a missionary to work amongst the town's poor. Joseph's reputation was well known to one of the leading figures in the congregation, Thomas Paget, the surgeon, and he was accordingly offered the position at a salary of £75 per annum.[2] He accepted and the family took up residence in a house belonging to the Great Meeting, at 122 Churchgate, almost directly opposite St Margaret's Church.[3] Joseph remained in the position of domestic missionary till 1876, when ill-health forced his retirement. He died in 1883.

The Origins of the Leicester Domestic Mission

The Leicester Domestic Mission was set up by local Unitarians in 1845 in All Saints' Open, opposite All Saints Church on Highcross Street. Though a small sect, the Unitarians were the most closely-knit and influential political body in the town. Subsequent to municipal reform in 1836, they provided the new borough of Leicester with its first seven mayors. In consequence, the Great Meeting Chapel became known as the 'Mayor's Nest'.[4]

Joseph Dare

The Leicester Unitarians had not conceived the notion of the 'domestic mission' by themselves. They had been influenced by the work of Dr Joseph Tuckerman (1778-1840), who served as 'Minister at Large' between 1826-39, from the Domestic Mission he had established in Boston, Massachusetts, USA.[5]

Tuckerman deplored the increasingly materialistic nature of society, particularly the uncaring attitudes it bred and the inequitable distribution of wealth it engendered. He was interested in the 'neglected poor' in cities. He sought to remove the underlying causes of social deprivation and discontent. He demanded increased state legislation over these issues yet objected strongly to the state's provision of social institutions with their impersonal character. He asserted that the local community had to bear the responsibility of caring for its poor: 'It is the city which should discharge a parent's duty,' he maintained. Both local municipal and voluntary agencies would be involved in the process. In consequence, Tuckerman contended, local governing elites would recover their sense of duty by ministering to the social and moral needs of the poor, and the latter, in turn, would re-learn the virtues of self-reliance and disciplined living.

Dr Joseph Tuckerman

Class prejudices would be broken down and a more sustained and deliberate effort towards social integration achieved.

Tuckerman's thinking was rooted in an immanentist theology in which the Divine was seen to be acting through the historical process. It implied a sincere belief in the organic nature of society, in which the social and the spriritual, the physical and the mental, progressively interplay, slowly yielding, through their mutual antagonism, to an eternally advancing Reason. It represented a free theology imbued with a sound definition of the minister's calling. The concept of the Domestic Mission was both the practical outcome and the testament to this theology.

Tuckerman had visited England in 1833-4 and established Missions on the Boston model in London and Liverpool. Subsequent ones were set up in Manchester, Birmingham, Bristol, Leeds and Leicester.[6]

The *raison d'être* of these Missions was recognition of the increasing physical, social and moral problems associated with nineteenth-century urbanization - the 'contagion of numbers'[7] - combined with a desire to do something about them. Leicester's ruling elite was well aware of the increasing demographic problem - the period 1801-41 had seen the town's population increase from about 17,000 to 50,932.[8] This, coupled with the general distress prevalent amongst local framework knitters[9] - the staple employment - and the increasing presence of Chartist activists in the town,[10] had caused concern. The establishment of the Leicester Domestic Mission represented one important response to that concern.

The Annual Reports of the Leicester Domestic Mission, 1846-77

At the end of each year's work in his capacity as domestic missionary, Joseph Dare produced a *Report* for the benefit of the Mission's benefactors.[11] Today, these *Reports* - which amount to some 400,000 words - have wider significance as an invaluable source for social and urban historians of the Victorian age. Their importance is three-fold: in the first place, they afford valuable insight into the way a domestic mission operated in its dealings with the working classes, how it defined its aims and how it went about realizing them; secondly, the *Reports* catalogue the major changes the town underwent in the period, particular attention being paid to the efforts made by both local authorities and voluntary agencies to improve the physical, social and moral well-being of the working classes; finally, and perhaps most important of all, the *Reports* provide an invaluable longitudinal account of working-class life-styles, based on Dare's first-hand experience and observations.

The book is divided into two main sections. Section I deals with the work of the Leicester Domestic Mission. Section II is devoted to working-class life and the local efforts undertaken to improve the quality of that life. This section consists of five main chapters: Employment, Poverty and Charity; Environment and Health; Education; Recreation; Religion. Commentary is interspersed with representative extracts from the *Reports*, the selection being made to take account both of changing conditions and the temper of Dare's outlook.[12] The overall aim is to present a picture of Leicester's working classes in the period 1845-77. It is a picture based on the perceptions and attitudes of one local Victorian middle-class commentator. It represents one man's attempt to understand and explain what was, in many respects, an alien culture. As such, it reflects the inner tensions and conflicts, the tenuous unfolding, of the social philosophy of a local Victorian reformer.

Acknowledgements

Special thanks are due to several people for making the publication of this book possible: Dr David Reeder, of the Urban History Centre, Leicester University, for his encouragement; the staff of Leicestershire Libraries, especially Mr Aubrey Stevenson, Ms Jane Hipwell and Mr Dipak Chauhan for seeing the book through publication; Leicestershire Museums and the *Leicester Mercury* for their assistance in the provision of photographic and illustrative material; Mrs Linda Barker for her speedy and efficient word-processing; my wife, Pauline, for her painstaking proof-reading; my son, Richard, for his patience; and, of course, Joseph Dare, a most remarkable man, to whose memory the book is dedicated - indeed whose book it is.

Gallowtree Gate, 1847

Section I

THE WORK OF THE LEICESTER DOMESTIC MISSION

The Leicester Domestic Mission

The 'Committee's Report' for 1852 defined the scope of the Leicester Domestic Mission:

It is well to keep constantly in view the object aimed at. In every populous town there is a large amount of ignorance and vice; of want, imprudence and sorrow; multitudes are destitute of the elements of morality and religion, and seldom, or never, enter a place of worship.[1]

The overall aim of the Leicester Domestic Mission was consequently to mitigate these great 'evils'. Joseph Dare spoke of the need:

to relieve emergency, to comfort the sick and dying, to awaken self-energy, self-reformation, and faith in the goodness of our Father in heaven, to instruct those especially who have been neglected and improve as much as may be their physical and social condition.[2]

The neglected were specified by Dare in his 1849 *Report* as:

those touched by no other ministration - the sick and dying, the aged, the vicious and despised, those hopeless and reckless from the recollection of early wasted energies and misapplied powers.[3]

Consistent with Unitarian commitment to freedom of thought, the hallmark of the Mission approach was not dogmatist, 'narrow and sectarian'.[4] Joseph Dare tells us in 1848 that he did not resort to:

popular methods of reaching the poor: no flaming handbills, no proselytizing, no slandering of fellow christians.[5]

Dare had great faith in human nature and believed that even the most depraved and vicious could be reached through tolerance, love and kindness rather than censure.[6]

In order to achieve its objectives, the provision of educational classes for both sexes and all ages was deemed of paramount importance. Dare's 1846 *Report* details the educational activities underway during the Mission's first year of operation:

The Committee have fitted up an excellent room in All Saints' Open for educational purposes. A Sewing School; an Adult Class, for men; a Boys' and Girls' Class - on separate evenings; a Reading Room, Library, and Sunday school, have been established, and attended from their commencement with various but decided success. The Sewing School meets weekly on Monday and Tuesday afternoons. It was opened on Nov.10th,1845, with sixteen children, and there has been an average attendance ever since of not less than from forty to fifty, except during the harvest weeks. This number might be doubled or trebled at any time. It gives me great pleasure to state that this branch of the Mission is admirably conducted by those ladies who kindly attend, in rotation, to impart instruction in this necessary art. The fact that there are hundreds of mothers, and their children, totally ignorant of this useful and necessary acquirement, will show the great utility of this institution. Several intelligent operatives have alluded to the want of this knowledge as being the source of much discomfort...This branch of the Mission, therefore, is effecting great good, not only in imparting practical knowledge, but in being made the means of enforcing habits of cleanliness and self-respect, as well as industry. Occasionally, some juvenile story is read over to the youthful listeners, and its moral pointed out, as they go on with their work. A pence-club has been some time in operation in this department. The children can lay out their savings on articles made in the school at merely nominal prices, or withdraw their deposits in money, if so required.

The Boys' and Girls' Evening Instruction Society has been attended by numbers varying from eighty to more than a hundred, except during the very hot weather, and then, indeed, the girls were scarcely diminished. The ages of the female attendants vary from eight or ten to between thirty and forty. Several of the visitors of the Sewing School have kindly officiated as teachers in the Girls' Instruction Society, and it is earnestly to be hoped that they will continue their kind and essential services. Thanks are especially due to the Misses Froane, and the Misses Weston, who attended nearly through the whole of the winter. May reflection on its great importance induce them to continue their laudable exertions. Ladies, who have brought up families, might render incalculable service by coming forward and giving hints to the children of their poorer sisters in the management of domestic affairs, and the peculiar duties that will one day devolve upon them, whether they are fitted to discharge them or not. Many an industrious man is made unhappy, and at last a drunkard, through the untidiness and waste of his slatternly wife, who is, at the same time, more an object of commiseration than censure - never having been taught the duties of her position.

The boys' department has been well supplied with teachers. It is saying but little towards the just estimation of the indefatigable exertions of these gentlemen, to state, that without their able and increasing co-operation, it would have been impossible to have progressed so far, and so satisfactorily, as we have done the first year.

The Adult Class for men was opened on Feb. 6, with eleven attendants; in three weeks the

Highcross Street c.1880. The Leicester Domestic Mission was situated on All Saints' Open, opposite All Saints' Church

number averaged from forty to sixty, till the fine weather. They are now again setting in for the winter, as the usual average attended last week. Their ages are from eighteen up to "grey hairs." The instruction hitherto attempted consists of reading, writing, arithmetic, geography, and familiar illustrations of the arts and sciences. For reading books we use at present the 1st, 2nd, 3rd, and "Moral Class Book" of Chambers' Educational Course, the Fourth Book of Lessons for the use of the Irish National Schools, the Life of Christ and the Holy Scriptures. Other little works are occasionally used as text books, for an introduction to useful knowledge, in art or science.

The Adult Class meets on Monday evenings, the boys on Tuesday and Wednesday and the girls on Thursday and Friday evenings.

It has been my aim to secure, if possible, the attendance of those who have been wholly neglected. This probably will have been surmised by the humble character of the instruction given. Many, in all the classes, knew not a letter at their first entrance; and there is a portion of children, called "Winders," who are so occupied that they are almost entirely cut off from the means of getting any kind of instruction. They are employed from very early in the morning till late at night; so late that they cannot attend our evening Instruction Society, though it is not closed till nearly ten o'clock. Brickmakers, clay-servers, and climbing boys are also almost wholly neglected. The improvement of a few in the Adult Class is very gratifying. The wife of one of them told me "the happiest portion of her life was that since her husband took to learning." Many who are fathers of large families manifest quite a child-like earnestness and simplicity in their desire for knowledge. How much this class is needed may be seen from the fact that great numbers can scarcely read - more cannot write; and, even amongst those who profess a knowledge of these things, the great majority can only read and write imperfectly - very few are acquainted with the common rules of arithmetic.

A Provident Society has been opened in both the boys' and girls' department; and the School exercises each evening are concluded with a short moral address, or by reading some appropriate tale, or singing a devotional hymn. These arrangements have produced a decidedly beneficial effect. More than one hundred have become depositors; the deposits vary from one penny to one shilling and sixpence. About ten pounds have been deposited in the whole, of which sum one third has been withdrawn with a small allowance of interest. Mrs. W. Biggs has kindly consented to become Treasurer. The singing is managed very pleasingly, and the address listened to with attention.

The Reading Room in All Saints' opened in May, and bearing in mind that the summer time is not the season for in-door relaxation, it promises well. There are, generally, from twelve to twenty sitting at the papers or periodicals, while some are passing out, and others are supplying their places. The literary fare, last week, consisted of the Morning Chronicle, supplied by W. Biggs, Esq.; Daily News, by T. Paget, Esq.; Inquirer, by J. Whetstone, Esq.; People's Journal, by W. H. Walker, Esq.; The Times, for the day, Leicester Mercury, Critic, and several provincial papers by Mr. G. Smallfield; Douglas Jerrold's Newspaper, and Leicester Chronicle, by E. Gittens, Esq.; Athenaeum, by B. Smith, Esq.; Chambers' Journal, Tau, &c. from the Periodical Society: Temperance Gazette, by G. S. Kenrick, Esq.; Punch, by Mr. Mills; besides duplicates of some of the local papers, &c. The whole of these useful works are supplied, and the room opened free of expense to the working classes, from seven till half-past ten o'clock every Saturday Evening.

The Library was commenced at the same time; it consists at present of nearly one hundred volumes; comprising about 30 volumes from Knight's Weeklies, presented by the committee; nearly the complete set of Miss Martineau's Illustrations of Political Economy, with other works, from Miss Paget; about twenty vols. of Travels and Biography, given by Mrs. Marillier; Evenings at Home, and other books, from Mrs. Parker, Worcester; five excellent vols. from Miss Brewin; three vols. from Mr. Mills; and a quantity of Chambers' Tracts and Journals from Miss Froane. The Periodical Society have also kindly allowed their works to be deposited here after circulation. Several volumes are issued weekly on which the nominal charge of one halfpenny each is made. T. Paget, Esq. will kindly add the "Barker Library," as soon as its publication is commenced. This will be a very valuable donation, as it will, doubtless, be the means of spreading nobler and more rational views of humanity and religion. The neglected masses may be won to any faith that comes to them accredited with acute benevolence and disinterested exertions for their physical welfare. Donations of books, on any subject, suited to man, as an immortal being, are earnestly solicited. Books of Travels, Biography, Natural History, Domestic Economy, &c. are most frequently enquired after.

The Sunday School was commenced July 13th. As it is intended to admit only those who do not attend any other Sunday School, the accession of numbers will be a work of time. I find, from my Journal, that five came the first Sabbath, twelve the next, and thirty on the third Sunday. But here again, irregularity of attendance, as in the other branches of the Mission, is the great obstacle to improvement. One third, at least, in each department, have disappeared, and others have filled their places, not less, perhaps, than three times over since the opening of the schools. This is a great evil, and can only be remedied by visiting and admitting as far as possible, only the children from localities adjacent to the place of tuition. The negligence of parents in this respect is very discouraging. Yet let us not despair of doing good; though some remain with us only for a short time, others persevere. Individuals have been kept from wickedness merely from recollecting one word or one lesson imparted in early life. It is a fearful task to shake off habits that have been long indulged.[7]

Dare also regarded Sunday public worship at the Mission as essential. By 1851, it appears to have been well established:

The attendance at the Mission Chapel has been very cheering through the whole of the year, though many have felt the pressure of the season, and been obliged to pledge some of their best garments, yet the services have been well attended. Even in the hottest weather our room has presented an animating group of earnest listeners. Many may now be called my regular hearers, applying to me in all cases of a religious nature. I have administered baptism, and officiated at the interment of several at our solemn and beautiful Cemetery. I have not as yet been able to secure the attendance of many, at least in any regular manner, belonging to the Sunday School or other branches. Numbers of them are too young, and the grown up ones like to go where they may "see and be seen:" but if we only teach them to read the Holy Scriptures, and to imbibe a love for public worship, our labours will not be thrown away. Individuals belonging to the other branches occasionally attend, but the chief part of the audience are those I visit, or the parents of children taught in some of the classes. Some few after attending awhile seem to crave for exercises more exciting: they make religion consist of passion and feeling alone. Their spiritual aspirations are merely emotional, and hence it is to be feared that ultimately they relapse again into their old habits; others I have observed - and three in particular recur to my recollection - who, after being awakened to a sense of religion, take a different view of life altogether. These three have been rabid democrats and socialists, but are now convinced that the general welfare of the race must chiefly arise from individual improvement, and the spread of the Gospel and the spirit of Christ. This view I labour to extend. Public devotion is a powerful means of doing it. The poor especially require social worship to sustain them under privation and suffering; their homes are too often scenes of discomfort; neighbours are slanderous and quarrelsome; but in the house of prayer worldly associations are forgotten, differences laid aside, and faith and hope strengthened by spiritual intercourse.[8]

A department was also set up at the Mission to distribute tracts on social, sanitary and moral matters to the working classes. In 1862, Dare referred to some important ones:

The Sheffield and Hull tracts, and those issued by the "Ladies' Sanitary Committee," are doing a good service. I called one day on the father of a family to whom I had lent a tract on "The Value of Good Food, &c." He seemed to think that it must have been designed for parties altogether above the working man, and was half inclined to bring out a new tract on the subject from his own point of view. I advised him by all means to do so, as it would be useful, not only to his own class, but also to correct the judgement of the author of the one in question. Another of these tracts caused a mother to throw open her beds and windows daily. The head of another household brought out some of the Sheffield tracts expressing how much pleasure they imparted. Judicious tracts, rational tracts, whether upon religion or social matters, are

Joseph Whetstone, a local worsted manufacturer, a leading Unitarian and long-standing Committee member of the Leicester Domestic Mission, and a key figure in local politics

read by the thinking man. But I believe the common religious tracts are very little thought of; they are taken in from courtesy, but returned without being properly read.[9]

Throughout his *Reports* Dare described the progress made by each of the Mission branches, noting in particular any changes being made or any special problems. 'One great obstacle to improvement in any of the classes,' wrote Dare in 1846, 'is irregularity of attendance.' He lists some major reasons for it:

This seems, in part, occasioned by shifting from one house to another. In my short experience I have known a great number of families remove; some more than once; some three or four times; and one family I know have changed their abode six times in as many months. Sickness and scarcity of work at some periods, and exhaustion from labour at other seasons, also cause irregularity, and many of the poor little things fall asleep over their lessons. Some are precluded from regular attendance through the want of shoes, or outer garments; and some, I fear, are drawn away by early vice.

It strikes me that the chief reason why many of the grown-up attendants fall away, is the inaptitude always felt upon entering upon new undertakings: the difficulty is present and apparent - the good remote and unappreciated. The process of learning seems tedious and the progress slow; so that after a few attempts they disappear; and hence I infer that Infant Schools may be made more beneficial than they now are, by imparting to every child attending, at the earliest possible season, a practical knowledge of reading and writing, if only the single letters and figures, instead of spending all the child's time in merely repeating pieces it can never read. I find that adults who have gained ever so little practical knowledge in their childhood, can be more easily induced to attend instruction than those who have not enjoyed this advantage.[10]

'Paucity of efficient teachers', wrote Dare in 1846, was a particularly major problem. Indeed he deemed it:

the great evil of all kinds of educational establishments for the poor of the present day. This remark applies both to secular, and Sunday Schools. The number of scholars is pointed to as a proof of success rather than the manner in which they are taught, or what they learn. The poor require the best of teachers. Their habits, thoughts, feelings, actions, all want continual and kindly guidance.[11]

In 1854 Dare additionally noted:

how scarcely any working men, who had been improved in the Mission, come forward to assist in teaching their less instructed fellows.[12]

The Boys' Class persistently proved the most difficult to manage. Dare regularly blamed this on a variety of factors, notably: laxness of parental control and the indifference of parents to the education of their offspring; early and exhausting toil, contrasted by long periods of involuntary idleness; brutality and wickedness experienced in many workshops and warehouses; and evil companionship. Dare highlighted the problem most cogently in 1849:

A large portion of this class may be fairly denominated "ragged," as many of them are the off-spring of poor widows, or the brothers of individuals who are improving under our silent system, or working out their redemption in the penal settlements. I find from my monthly reports that the number of boys has varied from forty to eighty. This has been caused partly by fluctuations in employment, and partly by a paucity of teachers. This instructional branch, though one of the most important, is in the least satisfactory state of all the departments of the Mission. Numerous applications for admission are constantly refused on this account. The teaching has almost wholly devolved upon the Missionary, and his kind friend, Mr. Geo. Mills. The rude and undisciplined conduct of the boys shows in a fearful manner their ignorant and depraved condition. Neglected and brutalized in their daily callings, it is a great labour to awaken in them any sense of moral discipline or recognition of the law of love. Still, improvement is perceptible in those who are regular in attendance. And that kindness is the only means of governing them may be seen in the pleasing fact, that having been obliged to request three individuals to withdraw till promise of better behaviour, they all returned the next week, and in a very subdued manner begged to be re-admitted. Of course this was granted, as this was the only object of sending them away. They have behaved better ever since. When will every place of worship throughout the land have its "ragged school"? It is the neglect of this class that is the sole cause of the greater part of the vice and irreligion of which the May gatherings in London, and Bible Societies, and other similar institutions, complain. Till their social and moral condition be properly attended to, so as to awaken self-reliance and self-respect, society will be infested with the drunkard, the beggar, and the felon. Vice, irreligion, and disease, are the retributions of neglect. Nor is anything gained in a pecuniary point of view by "shuffling off" this labour. It was stated in that excellent paper, the Gateshead Observer, a short time since, that "eleven children belonging to Newcastle cost the borough no less than £387. 17s. 7d. for their maintenance in prison, having been committed nearly twenty times." Does not every borough afford similar cases? - On the first Tuesday this month, nearly 100 boys applied for admission. But the number must be reduced, or more teachers supplied. As a class, the "Winders" are in the worst moral condition.[13]

By contrast, the Girls' Class was generally much better attended and behaved. 'As may be expected,' Dare wrote in 1846, the girls are 'more docile and tractable'.[14] The increasing numbers attending the Girls' Class soon led Dare to create a separate Female Adult Class. Its progress is reported in 1850:

This class has fully sustained its average attendance, the numbers being rather higher in winter, and less in summer, than in the corresponding seasons of last year. It is to be regretted that the young women cannot assemble till quite eight o'clock. Miss Brewin recently presented them with a set of very nice class books. They have gone through them several times, and are much pleased with them; the set being a selection of moral sentences from a number of our best authors. Many applicants in this branch have to begin by learning their letters. Their general progress is very encouraging. Several, who could scarcely write a letter when admitted, copied, as a dictation exercise on the slate, a verse or two of 'How doth the little busy bee,' &c., in a very tolerable manner. The first class use two of the British School books, which are of a superior description, and have occasional lessons in English history. About 120 went on the second Wednesday in February to the exhibition of the Fine-Art Union. They were admitted at half-price, one penny each; and they were greatly delighted with the pictures. Their criticisms were quite amusing. Such exhibitions awake true taste, and afford innocent recreation. I think there have not been so many individual changes as occurred last year. Hence their improvement is manifest. From four to six distinct exercises are generally gone through each evening. The whole business is concluded as formerly, with singing and prayer. Myself, Geo. Mill, and James Winters, are the teachers, with occasional assistance from the first class.[15]

Changes were also made to the Mission Sunday School in 1858:

Our Sunday school consists now of two distinct branches. The elder classes are taught in the morning from ten until twelve o'clock, and the younger from two till four in the afternoon. The morning class has averaged between sixty and seventy during the year, which is scarcely so many as our usual number. The non-attendance has been chiefly amongst the adult members, occasioned by pressure of employment. The over-wrought frame has required additional rest, and this has been taken on the morning of the Sabbath. The fearful amount of sickness, too, that afflicted us last autumn, caused many to be occasionally absent.

With this temporary fluctuation the classes assembling in the morning exhibit encouraging signs of regularity and improvement. The classes meeting in the afternoon are in every respect a most important and efficient part of our labours. This branch was commenced about a year ago by way of experiment. Observing many children in the neighbourhood of the school who were poorly clad, and who, it appeared, did not attend any Sunday school, they were invited to come to the mission room on Sunday afternoons.

This invitation met with a hearty response. From twenty to thirty at once presented themselves, and this number has gone on increasing, till the average attendance has for some time been about seventy. This branch is designedly for the humblest grade of children, and many of the poor little things had been rejected at other Sunday schools because they were not dressed sufficiently well. They are admitted at the earliest age. Every Sunday school should have an infant department, as by this means, not only the tender mind is brought under moral training at the earliest possible season, and before vicious habits have been contracted, but the elder children can be better spared to attend if the infant portion of the family are in safety. It is obvious too, that if this branch be well managed it becomes a feeder to the older classes. There are writing and sewing classes, a library and provident club in connection with our Sunday school. Four teachers attend in the morning and six in the afternoon who are very regular in their attendance, and their persevering efforts, under the blessing of our Heavenly Father, have been rewarded by encouraging signs of success.[16]

Changes were also made to the Mission's juvenile instructional programme following the 1870 Education Act. Acknowledging the greater effectiveness of the Board School system, Dare accordingly wrote in 1875:

In presenting my Thirtieth Annual Report it is very cheering to find that some of the labours of the Mission have been superseded, and some of our aims realized, by the improved social conditions of certain portions of the community; and more particularly by the institution of Board Schools, where, even the hitherto neglected children, for whom several branches of the Mission were carried on, may now be more fully taught and trained.

The same reasons that properly led to the closing of the schools at the Great Meeting apply more strongly to the branches of the Mission for the mere elementary instruction of juveniles of school age. When we commenced our labours, there were some thousands of wholly neglected children wandering at large, without the possibility of attending any means of instruction, as, if from no other cause, there was not efficient school accommodation for half their number. Happily this is no longer the case; there are now six excellent Board Schools open in the town. It will, therefore, be a better service to induce such children to attend efficient schools, than attempt to instruct them in any other way during school age. The efforts of sectarians are often unavoidably irregular, spasmodic, and inefficient, as, of course, properly certificated teachers cannot be secured for such purposes.

In connection also with this subject I received a communication from Mrs. E. H. Paget, the kind superintendent of the sewing branch. It was found that the attendance was fluctuating, and that nearly the whole of the little sewers had become pupils of the Board Schools, and, as needle-work is systematically taught in those establishments, it would be better to encourage them to attend the Board Schools, than to divide their attendance between two institutions, which no doubt would often lead to non-attendance at either, and thus frustrate the object of both. "In fact," as Mrs. Paget justly concludes, "we should only be working against the School Board."

Our labours, then, amongst the little ones of school age, who were formerly so sadly neglected, are no longer required. A new order of things has made ample provision for their educational rights and necessities, fully realizing the views we entertained thirty years ago. Personally I feel much rejoiced, as my hopes for the improvement, and elevation, and happiness of the working classes are chiefly based on their being properly trained and instructed in their childhood. We may rest assured now that in due time this will be accomplished, for the Home Secretary has manfully declared: "You cannot in any reason suppose that a man who has the power of sending his child to school has a right to neglect to teach him, any more than he has to neglect to feed or clothe him. If he does not do it, he must be made to do it."[17]

Evening classes at the Mission were subsequently closed to all those of school age.

Unlike the moribund local Mechanics' Institute, the Mission from the start encouraged the active participation of its working-class members. Working men and women were consequently given the opportunity to voice their own opinions and practise their own powers and talents wherever possible. The Discussion Class for men was early established on the 'mutual instruction' principle with questions and discussions being invited from working-class members. The intention behind the measure together with a list of topics discussed - typical of those given throughout the *Reports* - are noted by Dare in 1850:

There has been a regular attendance in this branch, of more than twenty. Considerably more than a hundred individuals have occasionally attended, and the above average was sustained even in the hottest months. This class affords an opportunity of becoming acquainted with the real sentiments and opinions of the operatives. Unbelief and Socialistic notions prevail amongst many of them. The majority of a certain grade mock at all the religious systems of the day. They have no reverence for religionists, and no faith in doctrines that seem to produce but little effect in modifying the evils of society. Discussion classes, if managed with care, might be the means of spreading sounder views upon the various subjects on which the operatives feel strongly, without possessing much correct information. They act as a kind of safety-valve to let off exasperated feelings and to modify erroneous opinions.

Many important subjects have been discussed. The following are examples of some of them. "What are the best means of self-improvement?" "What are the best means of making Mechanics' Institutes available to the working classes?" "What are the effects of Free Trade?" "Are Capital Punishments justifiable?" "Socialism as propounded by Robert Owen?" "What are the effects of the Law of Primogeniture and Hereditary Legislation?" "Are the Peace-schemes practicable?" &c. The questions are proposed, as nearly as possible, by the whole of the members in rotation. Each person is at liberty to speak in his turn for ten minutes, or to pass his turn without speaking. There is no surer way of

Samuel Stone, a founder Committee member of the Leicester Domestic Mission and Town Clerk in the period

eliciting their ideas and feelings. It is a key to the mind. When that is unlocked, knowledge may be applied more effectually.[18]

Increasingly, outdoor pursuits were added to the scope of the Discussion Class. By 1874, Dare referred to how:

The annual walk to Charnwood and the picnics of our singers and reciters at New Parks, Beaumont Lodge, and Birstall Holt were greatly enjoyed; they so seldom breathe the fresh air or gaze upon the blue sky. They will remember they are to go again when the "broom is in flower."[19]

To improve working men's knowledge, lectures on scientific subjects were also initiated.[20] 'The botanist has a harmless and useful hobby,' wrote Dare in 1867.[21] A 'Window Plant Show' was commenced in 1868, enabling working men to display the results of their labours:

As the mind requires change and amusement, and as healthful and harmless hobbies have great influence in forming personal habits, we added this year a Window Plant Show to our other branches. Dogs and rabbits, fowls and pigeons, birds, ferrets, and guinea pigs, in confined dwellings, create filth and disease, besides being the cause of annoyance to others; but the culture of a plant or flower requires light, and air, and sunshine, and freedom from smoke and dust, repaying the care bestowed with beauty and fragrance, and tending to produce a more healthful atmosphere. The following notice of our first attempt is encouraging: "On Wednesday, August 12th, this extempore flower show took place, and made so fair a start that its success as an annual institution is certain. About a hundred plants in pots were brought in from various nooks and corners in the neighbouring streets. W. Evans, Esq., and G. H. Wade, Esq., both of Belgrave, and Mr. Foster of the Cemetery, contributed a number of fine specimens to add to the effect of the show, as well as cut flowers for ornamentation and small plants for distribution as prizes. Mr. Hepworth sent cut roses from his fine collection, and the Misses Wade and Evans bunches of wild flowers and many coloured berries. Among the plants for competition, fuchsias, scarlet geraniums, and myrtles, were the most numerous; but there were also a large cactus, a nicely grown crassula, a mimulus cardinalis, two begonias, several scented geraniums, a succulent saxifrage, and various other species. One working man, who cultivates a garden on the Common sent a splendid basket of cut roses, verbenas, and gladioli, while another, who prefers the garden which nature cultivates for us all, and spends his leisure in the study of local botany, had constructed a curious kind of tree, from bunches of our Leicestershire grasses, about two dozen species being represented in it. Mr. Foster and Mr. Mott took the part of judges, and it was agreed that in this first attempt there should be no blanks. The specimens of each exhibitor were judged by themselves, and a first, second, third, or fourth class prize awarded, according to the merits of each group. The show is to be carried out more completely next season. We wish it all success, for there is nothing which preaches more loudly to a utilitarian age than a well-grown plant, and no ornament more desirable for the cottage window." From the interest manifested, there is no doubt that another year will fully realize our design. Many wished they had known of this earlier, and determined to prepare for the next.[22]

Throughout the period the Mission made increasing provision for social gatherings and tea-meetings, in the belief that they would have 'some influence in forming the general mind for more rational amusements'.[23] Dare maintained that the provision of rational recreations was imperative in order to counteract 'questionable' working-class relaxations like drinking. He claimed to have been the first in the town to have initiated 'Penny Concerts', consisting of music and recitations carried on by the workers themselves.[24] In 1865, Dare reported:

We gave ten literary and musical entertainments, or "Penny Readings," as they are called. They were all crowded and carried on by the operatives themselves. I think greater efforts should be made to induce the workers to take part in such performances, instead of the more educated keeping them nearly altogether in their own hands. If better tastes are to be awakened amongst the neglected, they must be encouraged to try their powers, and not to be merely listeners. Of our entertainment in January, it is recorded in my journal: "One circumstance afforded me much pleasure. A smart lad, who had been very difficult to manage in the evening class, prepared a recitation at my request, and delivered it in a spirited manner, to the evident enjoyment of himself and his associates. I had taken him by the hand at the previous concert, and told him as he was fast growing into manhood he should join the adult class, and come forward and co-operate with us as he must now well know what our designs were." He came to the adult class, took part in the next concert, and has evidently "turned over a new leaf." This was the third "rough" we enlisted during the season. Another unexpectedly proffered a choice of recitations, including "Ginevra" or the "Mistletoe Bough," which he described as very touching. The celebration of Shakespeare's birthday afforded, as usual, another social and interesting meeting. It should have been stated last year that the commemoration of his ter-centenary afforded a small balance, with which we purchased a popular edition of his plays and placed them in the Town Hall Library, as a memorial of growing reverence for his name.

The tea meetings, with recitations and music, at the Races, at Christmas and the New Year, afforded much enjoyment, especially to those admitted by free tickets, who, but for these gatherings, have no means of mingling in social scenes; but the crowning re-union of the season was the "old men's feast." There were fifty-five present, and six who had become too infirm to attend had their dinners sent. In the course of the year five or six of the old men had "fallen asleep," but their places were readily filled up. Few indeed are left, who were at the first feast, sixteen years ago. Some present were eighty, ninety, or a hundred years of age, and none below sixty. They greatly enjoyed themselves, and passed a hearty vote of thanks to Mr. and Mrs. Walker, for their continued kindness to the "old and poor". [25]

From the beginning of the Mission's operation, emphasis was placed on making 'self-aid and self-reliance the rule and charity the exception'.[26] Nevertheless, a wide range of charity was made available, through the Mission's 'Relief Fund', to 'deserving' individuals with whom Dare was familiar. Each *Report* itemises the details of the 'Relief Fund', including the names of donors. In 1865, the following are listed:

Blankets: Mrs. J. Whetstone and T. Stokes, Esq. New Articles of Clothing: Mrs. Brewin (very useful and valuable parcel), Miss H. Stone, Mrs. Walker, Ladies Sewing Society, Miss Paget. Cast-off Clothing, Shoes, &c: Mrs. Wardle, Mrs. A. Paget, Miss Simpson, J. Whetstone, Esq. Lying-in Tickets: Mrs. Biggs, Mrs. Kempson, Mrs. T. Paget. In and Out Patient Tickets for the Infirmary: Mrs. Else, A. Paget, Esq., Miss. Spurrett, Mr. Ride, Mr. Pollard, Mr. W. Moore, E. Clephan, Esq., Misses White, Loughboro', Rev. Mr. Coe. Dispensary Tickets: W. Whetstone, Esq., Miss Brewin, Mr. W. Moore, E. Clephan, Esq., Miss Paget. Food, Wine, &c: Mr. Whetstone, Mr. Mott, who kindly allows what I wish for my patients. Tickets to the Wellington Dining Hall: Mrs. E. Paget (this is a very convenient form of relief. I found the tickets very useful.) Homoeopathic Tickets: Miss Brewin, Mrs. S. Stone. Free Tickets to Tea Meetings and Rural Fête: Mrs. S. Stone, Mrs. Stone, Rutland-street, Mrs. and Miss Spurrett, Mrs. T. Paget, Miss Smith, Mrs. A. Paget, Mr. Mott, Miss C. Paget, Mrs. T. T. Paget, Miss Brewin, Miss Burberry, Mrs. Ed. Paget, Mrs. Hodges, Messrs. J. Whetstone, R. Brewin, J. Silver, F. Johnson, Conyers Smith. N.B. Mission Station, to which books, or any articles useful to the poor may be sent, 122, Church-gate.[27]

Dare acknowledged that, though it was always best to enable the poor to help themselves, 'the difficulty is frequently in making the start'.[28] By giving charitable aid to the deserving, therefore, Dare felt he was placing them 'above the need of assistance'.[29] His period as missionary witnessed much recurrent poverty and distress amongst Leicester's working classes, when he felt it his duty to impart the charity he had at his disposal to those, whose 'quiet and patient suffering' called forth the 'kindest sympathy'.[30] The cases Dare considered to have prime claims were the sick, elderly and destitute. Consistent with his anti-proselytism, Dare did not make charitable assistance dependent on attendance at religious worship.[31] He regularly gave details of how Mission charity was distributed. In 1876 he noted:

All the cases relieved were old people; all of them afflicted in some way or other, and all sufferers from the late floods. Mrs. G., aged 70, living with an elder brother at No. 12, Ruding Street, Braunstone-gate, 2s. 6d. Mrs. T., nearly 70, has had to give up work through loss of sight, 2s. 6d. Mrs. C. and Mrs. B., two old ladies, living by themselves next door, both afflicted, old and very infirm. I left with them 3s. 6d. Mrs. S., New Park Terrace, an old lady, whose house had been flooded over the fire grate, and up to the window sill. I left with her 2s. 6d. The Misses

Sanvey Gate c.1880 - part of the area served by the Mission

H., living at No. 8, Foxon-street, two maiden sisters, one afflicted about two years with paralysis, the other having to wait upon her, 2s. Mrs. B., aged 76, living at No. 18, Foxon-street, afflicted now six years, 2s. 6d. Mrs. V., aged 90, a widow, living at No. 23, Foxon-street. I left with her 2s. Mrs. B., No. 55, Braunstone-gate, a widow, just recovering from a severe illness, aged 69, 2s. 6d.[32]

The success and usefulness of the Mission depended upon the ability, enthusiasm and character of the missionary. Joseph Dare was a wise choice for the role. The Committee of the Leicester Domestic Mission regularly acknowledged the fact in their short preamble to each *Report*. In 1846, for instance, the Committee paid tribute to the:

patient, unwearied and indefatigable performance of the onerous duties of his office.[33]

The 'distinctive feature' of the missionary's role, Dare wrote in 1847, was visiting the poor in their own homes.[34] He acted very much like a modern-day social worker, giving them 'advice, encouragement, consolation and assistance'.[35] He paid an estimated 4000 visits per annum, thus totalling well over 100,000 during his life's work.[36] He went to great lengths to keep in touch with families he knew well who had left the area, thus extending his visits all over the town.[37] He always appears to have been welcomed. No reports of physical assault are ever recorded. He worked long, arduous hours, personally supervising every aspect of Mission activity. The 'journal of a week's labours', which he wrote in 1854 - breaking from the usual manner in which he presented his *Reports* - illustrates the dedicated and conscientious manner in which Dare undertook his duties. It is particularly important for the detailed insight it gives into both the type of people he visited and the manner of his visits:

Monday. Called on: 1st.- a steady, hopeful family; several of the children have attended our classes. The eldest daughter and her female companion are desirous of attending again, now winter is returning. 2nd.- The parents here are methodists. Their little girl had been in our school some time and is now to attend the class on Thursday evening. 3rd. and 4th. - respectable families, some of whose members have occasionally attended the classes and divine service. 5th.- The parents, reform methodists. The wife advised by Mr. Paget to go into the Infirmary on account of bad foot and leg. But the husband suffers from ill health and she has a son, by a former husband, who earns a few shillings a week at a factory, so her natural affection struggles between the duty of going and her wish to attend to their comforts, and thus illness often becomes fatal. 6th.- a widow and constant attendant at the mission chapel. She recently lost, both at the same time, her orphan grandchild, in decline, and her husband, who had been bed-ridden from paralysis for more than a year. Originally a baptist, he had attended our service for several years. He was led to us in the first instance by curiosity but never left us afterwards till disabled by sickness. I constantly attended him till death released him to a better state, and was often strengthened in my labors, and in the assurance of their beneficial influence by his calm resignation and faith in the blessed promises of the gospel of Christ, which alone can give support and consolation when "heart and flesh fail." I gave the poor widow a trifle and left her with a thankful heart. 7th.- a household of three who all attend our Sunday Service as regular hearers. 8th.- methodists, but two of the children come to the girls' class. 9th.- absent. 10th.- an aged couple; their two daughters came formerly to the female adult class to learn to write, being also teachers at the same time amongst the association methodists. The husband, now nearly eighty, is a member of that body. Had a chat with him upon "election and reprobation," neither of which he could do with, he said. He is an example of the benefit of early moral training as though he witnessed much degradation while a soldier, he is now a prayerful and humble follower of Jesus and nothing gives him more delight than to talk of the mercy and goodness of God towards him. 11th.- a family I have known

Reverend C. Berry, minister of the Great Meeting Unitarian Chapel on Bond Street, 1803-59, and founder-member of the Mission Committee

for several years; they are religiously inclined and desirous of bringing up their children properly. They attend evening classes and the parents the Mission chapel. 12th.- this family had removed, so that I had not seen them a long time. I found the two eldest sons, who formerly attended the boys class, grown up. I invited them now to join the men's class. The parents were extremely glad to see me again, and thanked me warmly for the renewal of my visits. 13th.- respectable family, some of whose branches have assisted as teachers. As is usual in the evening I attended the Loan Office as a member of the committee; and from thence to the Men's Class.

Tuesday. 1st.- Wife sickly; supplied her with flannel petticoat from Ladies' Sewing Society. 2nd.- the parents in great anxiety about their son who was in the fearful battle of Alma. He had also been in the destructive engagement at Moultan where only himself and three others were left of a whole company. Two girls here, daughters, are, I am sorry to say, types of a numerous class in this town. The eldest has an illegitimate child, and the other scarcely in her teens, has withdrawn from our evening and Sunday school to attach herself to a youth about her own age. The most lamentable fact in relation to such conduct is that neither parents nor children seem conscious that it is wrong and the certain commencement of future want and misery. 3rd.- a laborer and teetotaler, his wife is, what every man's should be, clean, frugal, and industrious. They have five children; those old enough attend our classes or Sunday school; their parents go to the baptist chapel. The poor woman's last confinement was dangerous and she was reduced to great weakness. At my request a kind lady sent her strengthening food twice a week for some time. She often refers to this kindness with tears, as the means under God of raising her up again to the bosom of her family. Left a number of Buds and Blossoms for the children to read. 4th.- here resides a family just the reverse; the house is filthy, the children squalid and unruly, at school only once or twice in so many months. The parents do not seem to have either judgement or energy sufficient to manage their offspring. It would be a blessing to them and society if all such could be taken from their parents and placed in some reformatory institution. Left to grow up as they are, certain degradation is the consequence. The Penitent Home or the jail will then vainly attempt to reform them. 5th.- several members of this family formerly attended our adult classes and chapel. Some of them are now doing well in America, and in letters refer with thanks to our institution. 6th.- searched for parties who had given an address in this locality to a kind lady from whom they had solicited charity. This, like the majority of begging cases, proved to be a fabrication. I have enquired into several such cases during the year and have almost come to the determination of rejecting all applicants from the common lodging house and ready furnished room; there can be no reliance placed on their statements and where apparent affliction exists, the parties should be referred to their own parishes, and not allowed to hawk incurable diseases from one end of the country to the other, preying upon the means of private benevolence. Nos. 7, 8, 9, all steady industrious families; the father of one attended the adult class for some time, and some of the children of the whole come to their respective classes. I left amongst them some more Buds and Blossoms. No. 10, an old Sunday scholar; married and had had fits since her confinement; gave her a medical ticket. No. 11, the wife just discharged from the Infirmary; gave me the "return thanks" paper, and is to attend the mission chapel for that purpose. 12th, an old couple, the man, a second husband, is learning to read; I promised

Reverend C.C. Coe, minister of the Great Meeting Unitarian Chapel on Bond Street, 1855-74, and a long-standing Committee member of the Leicester Domestic Mission

to give him a suitable book, the wife fearing that one of the Buds and Blossoms would be rather too hard for him. She is a very worthy old woman and a striking example of the power of religion in the heart. She lost her first husband by a distressing malady and all their children. I think five, of consumption, after they had grown up. All but one came home to die. She nursed them with the tenderest care, patient and resigned to the will of God. In a previous visit I found her in trouble over the loss of some articles which had been purloined from her drawers, in her absence, by a relative who was leaving these parts. She "would not have minded" she said, "if she had not lost her shawl she went to chapel in." But she soon added "I forgive her, as perhaps she was in want." I promised her a flannel garment against winter and left her still hoping and cheerful. 12th, 13th, ordinary cases. 14th, 15th, gave one a shirt, and the other, a good old primitive methodist, enfeebled by age, a small trifle. Interred an infant at the cemetery. Called at the Sewing School. In the evening as usual I superintended The Boys' Class.

Wednesday. Of course the numbers used do not refer to the same families as above. No. 1 is a respectable household; two of the girls attend the female adult class. 2, 3, 4, ordinary cases. 5, 6,- the former I accompanied to take the pledge nearly two years ago. He has not been intoxicated since. He had been a violent Chartist; the last words he spoke to me were, "I see all reforms must begin at home." The latter keeps a small shop, she came to the evening class "to learn how to set things down." 7, 8, 9, 10, 11, 12, 13, ordinary cases. The last, an aged pair, requested me to get the husband of their youngest daughter to attend our men's class. He can neither read nor write. His wife is not much before him. Scarcely beyond childhood, of weakly frames, and with no certain occupation, they have already become parents of a sickly degenerate offspring. Too early marriage is a great evil. 14, here I was sorry to find that fever had swept off the father of a worthy family. He had frequently visited the mission room, and having read many excellent works, strove hard to spread more enlightened views amongst his fellows upon questions of labor and their social condition. His son was in the fever house, and there have been about thirty cases of this preventible malady in this street. A most filthy ditch runs along the bottom of it; the lower part of the next street was undrained and unpaved for years. I learnt that the sanitary officers had been to inspect this locality. In the afternoon I interred an adult at the Cemetery. In the evening, attended the Female Adult Class.

Thursday. Visited fifteen families to-day. None of these cases require especial comment except one, and in fact the particulars of this are too revolting for publication. I must pass them over. The father of this family, a confirmed drunkard, deserted them some years ago, and is now in Yorkshire, living with an abandoned woman. When I first became acquainted with the wife, she was in a despondent condition, through the unnatural conduct of her husband. I consoled her, and told her that she should not feel that, as self-degradation had been forced upon the family by one who should have been their protector. She gradually surmounted this feeling, and the children came occasionally to the classes. They suffered much privation. I attended the mother in her last illness at the Union, where she died. There are three orphans left. They are trying to keep the house on. Their position is a doubtful one. They promise to attend the class, when I hope to induce them to lodge with some elderly person. The other families I visited today were all well known to me. Some were of other denominations, some of no faith at all; but each gave me a friendly welcome, hoping I should soon call again. Some of their children attend our instruction, some wanted tracts, others I had attended in sickness, or performed for their deceased relatives the last sad office of interment. Attended in the evening The Girls' Class.

Friday. To-day I called on twenty-four families. Left at each house either a copy of the Economist, the Penny Sunday School Magazine, or a Bud and Blossom. These useful little works are looked for with great pleasure, and as they are often lent to other families, they are read by a great many persons. The excellent matter they contain must produce a good influence. They are often spoken of by others than of our denomination; and one old man, a good reader, is in the habit of gathering several persons together on a Sunday afternoon, to whom he reads the tale running through the Economist. Several mothers enquired for flannel garments and blanket-tickets against the winter, and to others I presented new articles placed at my disposal by Miss Biggs and the Misses Stone. At night I met the singers to go through the psalm tunes and other pieces, for divine service and our social meetings.

Saturday. I do not visit on this day unless sent for, which I frequently am, to attend the sick. I reserve Saturday to prepare for the Sabbath. In the evening, opened the Reading Room, and afterwards the Conversation Class. Neither has been once closed through the whole year.

Sunday. Our Sunday School is held in the morning from ten till twelve o'clock. As regards the educational condition of the scholars, it is mournful to see so many just verging on active life who can scarcely read. This absence of mere elementary knowledge renders our system of tuition more secular than should obtain in the Sabbath school. I see no remedy for it, except in the evening school, which should be attached to all Sabbath schools; and then the instruction in the latter might be as it ought to be, devoted wholly to religious subjects. There are four teachers besides myself in the Sunday school. Divine Service. This most important branch has been well attended the whole of the year; all my monthly reports refer to this gratifying fact. Several of the elder scholars attend. Others who come a long way are very regular.

Such, my christian friends, is a hurried sketch of the labors of a week. Such are the multiplied labors of another year, varied by the ever-changing circumstances of life. The various agencies in operation have all in a greater or less degree realized our designs. Under the blessing of our Heavenly Father, our work has prospered, and our boundaries have been enlarged. Prejudice has been conciliated, bigotry disarmed, the unenlightened instructed, the imposter detected, the suffering consoled, and the dying led to the promises of the blessed Redeemer.[38]

Dare, however, could not operate alone and he was supported by a large number of voluntary workers - particularly by those men and women prepared to help teach the various instructional classes and by those, like the Ladies Working Society, who collected and distributed second-hand clothing amongst the poor. Dare regularly referred by name to the many helpers and teachers who assisted him in the Mission's work, paying tribute, as he did in 1847, to their:

indefatigable exertions and their general kindness and influence over pupils, in softening the asperities arising from neglect, in cheering the monotony of uninterrupted toil, and imparting useful ideas.[39]

Without their able and increasing cooperation, the Mission's work would clearly have been impossible. Dare often acknowledged how he was personally encouraged in his own labours by their support and dedication.

As a voluntary agency, the Mission was also dependent on local subscriptions and donations. Familiar names from Leicester's elite gave financial backing to the Mission in addition to serving as Mission Officials. A list of the officials of the Leicester Domestic Mission during each year of operation - the President, Secretary, Treasurer and Committee Members - is given at the beginning of each *Report*. *Appendix 1* lists all these officials. *Appendix 2* gives some details of the Mission's financial accounts and subscribers as they appeared at the end of each *Report*.

Managing funds had to be exercised carefully. As an indication of how this was done, the following extract, which relates to the Sewing Class, serves as an interesting illustration. It was given by the retiring President of the class, Mrs T. Paget, and quoted by Dare in 1864:

It may be as well now to give you an account of the former and present state of our funds. We began with nothing. My first entry I find is for wash-hand basin, soap-dish, soap, towels,&c. We settled to sell the clothes made once a quarter, but at the commencement we had neither clothes, materials, nor money. But we managed to expend without funds. This continued till 1847, when it was arranged that we should receive £10 a year from the Mission funds. Of this sum you are aware £4 are paid for the cleaning of the Mission room, lighting the fire, &c., and £5 to the governess, leaving £1 for incidental expenses. We have now an ample stock of clothing and materials in hand; I should think at least six pounds' worth. We have also more than £20 in hand. This satisfactory result has been brought about by slow degrees, by a few kind presents of clothing from Miss Paget of Ibstock, Miss Biggs, and others, and about £3 from the sale of Miss Graham's patchwork quilts, and lately from a slight profit on the clothing sold. We shall have to decide what shall be done with this fund. I suggest that a portion shall be reserved. If cotton should by some unexpected chance ever fall as much and as rapidly as it has risen, there will probably be a slight loss on the stock in hand. Besides, if a time of distress should come, you would rather have the clothes sold under cost price. But doing every justice to my successor you may fairly reckon on having £15 at your disposal.[40]

Obtaining funds never appears to have been a problem, although by 1872, when the Committee issued the following notice, a shortage does seem evident:

The Committee of the Leicester Domestic Mission would venture to enforce upon its friends the necessity of increasing the number of the Subscribers, or of enlarging the amount of the subscriptions. The death or removal to a distance of some of the larger and more influential contributors renders it necessary that steps should be taken to maintain the society; and it is to be hoped that the good work will not be allowed to languish for want of funds. In this connexion the Committee beg to acknowledge with sincere thanks the liberal donation of their President (Harold Lees, Esq.,) by which the Society is freed from debt, and the generous assistance of T. T. Paget, Esq., whose recent contribution of £10 to the Relief Fund will afford a much needed help to one of the most useful branches of the Mission.[41]

Though the Mission did not seek public applause, it is clear that many locals and outsiders expressed approval of the beneficial work it did. Dare received many letters of gratitude from working men, indicating to him that the Mission was effecting some general good amongst the lower classes. Here is one such instance:

Gentlemen,

As a deputation from the various classes deriving advantages from your excellent institution, we beg to tender you our most sincere thanks and return the only sacrifice you would accept - the offering of grateful hearts. During the ten years the discussion class has been in existence, we not only have had the privileges of room, light, and fire, but have also experienced your liberality at our annual excursions and Christmas festivities, which convinced us that the same willing hands and generous hearts - though unseen - cared for our recreation as well as our mental elevation.

Your institution has ceased to be a theory and become an established fact; you have, through your faithful representative, sought out the depraved and neglected, and ministered to the pressing necessities of those who were unwilling to pass through the painful ordeal in order to obtain parochial relief, and thereby forfeit their independence; you have clothed the naked and fed the hungry, and poured the balm of consolation into the troubled heart, and infused into the sceptical better feelings, and convinced them of a religious reality.

Your Sunday and week-night schools have been attended with the most satisfactory results, and thousands will have cause to rejoice that they ever attended your room in All Saints' Open. The anxiety manifested by adults as well as children to obtain instruction (and in some cases unable for want of room) prove their willingness to learn when advantages, such as you so kindly offer, can be obtained. Such manifestations render it desirable that other similar institutions should be formed, seeing the harvest is plentiful and the labourers are few.

In conclusion, gentlemen, allow us again to thank you, on behalf of the various recipients of your Christian kindness, and to assure you, that however our various religious tenets may differ, we must ever reverence that religion which attends to the temporal as well as the spiritual requirements - the religion of the heart.[42]

It was not all smooth-running, however. 'Experience,' wrote Dare in 1855, 'is a mingled yarn of success and failure'.[43] Examples of both were regularly contrasted, as in 1847, for instance:

I have had several gratifying proofs of the moral effects of the Mission. A mother of three children informed me, with evident satisfaction, that her husband 'has quite altered his habits; he has left off drinking, and stays at home on Saturday nights.' Formerly, he spent their scanty earnings in drinking, causing them frequently, indeed almost always, to sit all day on Sunday with nothing to eat. He has already purchased two shirts from your society, and is now paying a few pence weekly for his children's clothing. Another, an old man, told me, when on a recent visit, that he had tried my advice of abstinence for nearly a month. He said he felt much better than he had ever done in his life. He had been a soldier, and a confirmed drunkard. He seemed quite delighted at the change; he is religiously inclined, and I have no doubt of his entire reformation. He has read many of our Tracts. 'What a sweet temper they are written in,' he exclaimed, when speaking of them. Two of his daughters, who could neither read nor write, have acquired both at the girls' school. Three or four others have obtained comfortable situations through my visits.

But there are many failures to discourage us. In contrast to the above I might point out the cases of four mothers who are addicted to drunkenness. They have fourteen or fifteen children amongst them; for the sake of these I call. Some of them come occasionally to our schools; but all is uncertainty and irregularity. Their parents sacrifice personal character - domestic comfort - the virtue even of their own off-spring, to procure the means of intoxication. When this vice lays firm hold, it is like the coil of the deadly serpent; destruction is almost inevitable. I weep "to give the record in," that thousands in the bosom of our boasted civilization seem too far sunk in degradation and wretchedness to respond to any ameliorating influences.[44]

One notable failure was the Mission 'Female Friendly Society', which Dare reported in 1855:

One of our branches, tried by way of experiment has failed. I have felt it necessary to dismember the "Female Friendly Society," for it turned out

John Biggs, a local hosier, Unitarian, supporter of the Mission, and a key figure in local politics in the period

anything but friendly. I had hoped to establish a society upon better principles than other female clubs, many of which in this town are held at public houses. It was commenced with the understanding that the rules should be modified as experience might suggest. This the members were unwilling to carry out though, from the fact that, either there is more sickness or more dishonesty amongst female members than amongst men; the run upon the box was altogether beyond the subscriptions. The least difficulty - the slightest cold - the scarcity of work even, was urged as a claim upon the funds. Neither was there a sisterly feeling, much less a religious spirit existing amongst them, though all meetings, according to the rules, were to be closed with prayer. As reason and remonstrance were alike ineffectual, I felt it would be best to dissolve the society. The funds were distributed amongst the members according to their time of entrance, some of the older ones receiving nearly £2 each. I have not quite given up the idea of forming another Female Friendly Society, being convinced that it would prove a most useful branch in the Mission. But if I make the attempt again it must not be with any drawn from the public-house clubs, but amongst those who have previously belonged to our classes or provident branches, and be wholly self-supporting.[45]

In addition, Dare often had to contend with a good deal of prejudice and bigotry against the Mission, its faith and methods, leading him to expose what he considered to be the 'slander and opposition of self-constituted censors'.[46] Many of these critics were clerics from other denominations. He considered their attacks in vain since his 'ministrations were continuously sought after.'[47] On this theme, Dare wrote in 1868:

Since our Mission was opened, twenty-three years ago, there have been more than a dozen ministers, vicars and curates, in the parish. With one or two exceptions, their chief and continuous efforts have been to obstruct our labours and to misrepresent our religious faith. They have not succeeded; their unchristian attempts only urge us to increased exertions, and secure us enlarged success. How is it possible that persons who stay so short a time, can become acquainted with the social and moral condition of the inhabitants? And why envy us the neglected children of the courts and hedges, who are not fine enough for their churches and confirmations, and who have been "despised and rejected," and turned out of their schools. We have teachers now in our Sunday school who were turned out of a Church Sunday school, lest the clothing of the poor little things should rub against silks and broad cloths. From whatever quarter unchristian bigotry may be manifested, I shall feel it to be my duty to protest against it. A short time ago a poor widow brought her two big boys, earnestly praying their admission, because they had lost their father and were so backward. We always make it a point to pay special attention to children deprived of their parents. They came to the Sunday school and evening class, and were making a fair start. But I soon missed them and on inquiring the cause of their absence, found that a person at whose factory they had just entered on work, told them they must go to the Church Sunday school; so these poor fatherless boys were deprived of their "writing and summing," and that, too, by one whose position arises from the kindness of a gentleman who was one of the first supporters of our mission. However, I requested the poor boys to attend the evening class as usual.

When the district nurses' institution was opened, I waited, at the request of a lady on its committee, on the Romish priest, to inform him of it, and to proffer tickets of recommendation to the nurses. I believe he has not used any, but as the nurses are for the sick and not the sectary, his non-co-operation will only widen our sphere of duty. Believing in no privileged order of priests, it seems to me simply unchristian not to unite in ministrations of benevolence. To all such we commend Dean Alford's manly and christian utterances: - "We are to be not unwise, but understanding what the will of the Lord is. And to my mind, His will has been unmistakably manifested in the free expansion of the christian conscience, as now found amongst us. It is our duty not to fight against His providence; not to attempt to work our way back to a uniformity which has utterly gone by; but to surrender our miserable jealousies; to accept bravely and frankly the state of things in which God has placed us; to walk in the kingdom of God, and to the house of God, and in society before the world, hand in hand with our Nonconformist brethren. Thus only shall we of the Church of England be making safe and wise preparation for the day which must soon come upon her. We may, if we please, lower ourselves, by exclusiveness and uncharitableness, so as to become in that day a mere sect amongst sects; but we may also, and I hope we shall, so lift in our esteem our christian brethren around us, as to find ourselves, when deprived of the State, a church amongst churches."[48]

The closure of All Saints' Mission in 1877 was a sad experience to all connected with the establishment. It marked the end of an era. Mr H.T. Basford, Dare's replacement as missionary in 1876, compared it to the 'leaving asunder of body and soul'.[49] Nevertheless, Basford maintained that there was still much social need for the Domestic Mission approach:

Less sensational preaching and more work is what we want; and, above all things, closer unity between classes. Caste is strong enough in England, and I pray God to bless the man who either by words or deeds puts his foot clean through the partition which divides class from class; and estranges the children of God from each other.

So far back as 1848 one of our Missionaries remarked, "Never has there been a time when Domestic Missions were more needed, or attention to the poor more needed on the part of the wealthy." And that cry may be repeated to-day. The poor working-man, often only partly employed, and shut out from every place of worship because his self-respect will not allow him to go in his work-day clothes, having no friend in whose ear he can pour his sorrowful tale, no one who can sympathise with him except a neighbour as poor, if not poorer than himself, gradually grows callous, and looks upon the rich man as his determined enemy, whose heel is ever upon his neck, keeping him down in the social scale. As poverty binds him down in a firmer grip, he begins to hate and detest the so-called upper classes of society. Such men view religion with distrust, and look upon the Missionary as one whose message it is to teach them "to be content in the condition in which it has pleased God to place them." They treat the Missionary with coldness at first; but, after a time, he finds his way to their hearts, and often, through the instrumentality of his wealthy friends, is able to give them a practical proof of the sympathy of the rich for the sufferings of the poor. It is a part of the Missionary's work to make the rich acquainted with the poverty of their less fortunate brethen, and then to bear their hand the response his message of sorrow has called forth.[50]

And, accordingly, Basford itemised a programme of activities for the coming year:

Every Sunday Evening at 6.30, Children's Church Service. Minister, Mr. H. T. Basford. Every Monday and Thursday Evening, Girls' School, 7.15 to 8.40. Teachers: Rev. J. P. Hopps, Mr. H. T. Basford, Mr. Sidney Gimson, Mrs. Hopps, Misses Lloyd, Miss Cotterill, Miss Fewkes, Miss Barradell, Miss Staples, Miss Whittle. Every Tuesday evening, Fife and Drum Band; 7 to 9. President, Mr. H. T. Basford. Every alternate Wednesday evening, beginning October 31st, recreation evening for young persons in Sunday and Mission Schools: conducted by Miss Clephan and Mr. J. M. Gimson. Every Friday evening, Boys' School. Teachers: Mr. A. J. Gimson, Mr. H. T. Basford. Every Friday evening, meeting of the Discussion Class at 8. Chairman, Mr. H. T. Basford. Every Saturday Afternoon at 3 o'clock, Sewing Class. President, Mrs. Hopps. Treasurer, Miss Else.[51]

The evening service, the Sunday school, the discussion and instructional classes were subsequently all removed to the Great Meeting Chapel buildings on Bond Street.

Section II

WORKING-CLASS LIFE

Introduction

At the heart of Dare's *Reports* are his detailed references to the life-styles experienced by Leicester's working classes. Coming into close daily contact with them for over thirty years in his role as domestic missionary, Dare was well placed to describe their condition. He felt passionately about the issue of working-class improvement, and in his first *Report* in 1846, he had echoed Tuckerman in arguing that the State had a duty to look after the physical, social and moral needs of the working classes:

It is truly said that "one half of the world does not know how the other half lives." A stranger passing through any of our larger towns, witnesses in one part busy streets lined with beautiful shops and handsome buildings - retired villas and walks promenaded by elegantly dressed inhabitants; but if he cast his eyes over another part, he will behold narrow and badly drained streets, filthy and confined courts; and their inmates, clothed in the same dress all the year through. These localities are thronged with unhappy beings, who from early and continued neglect, never arrive either physically or intellectually, at their proper stature. Great wealth is contrasted with extreme destitution, knowledge with the darkest ignorance, wisdom by folly, piety by wickedness.

This deplorable state of things has long awakened the sorrow and attention of the philanthropist, and is beginning to arouse the notice of the Government, in the maladministration of which, no doubt the cause will be found to originate... Whatever the poor are become, the nation, not to say the Government, is responsible for their condition: nor is anything gained, even in a pecuniary way, by neglecting them. If their physical wants are unsupplied, they must be fed as paupers - if their moral culture is overlooked they will grow up as "heathens in a strange land" - if they are not sent to school, many of them will become pupils under the silent system - if harmless recreations are not provided, strong drink and sensual indulgences will be resorted to - if they are suffered to reside in habitations unfit for human beings, fever and pestilence will stalk forth and desolate the neighbourhood.[1]

Dare accordingly demanded action - both local and governmental - to remedy all the 'great evils' which he associated with working-class existence: want of regular employment, want of early systematic instruction, want of better living conditions, want of rational amusements.[2] He defined this objective in collectivist terms, maintaining that the aim should be to ameliorate the 'general condition of the less favoured, and not merely to lift individuals above their class.'[3]

Corner of New Bond Street and East Gates c.1880

Dare regularly drew attention to the positive work being undertaken in the community towards improving the quality of working-class life. Yet praise could be very readily mixed with staunch criticism, as he detected shortcomings in the provisions being made. He regularly put forward recommendations as to what still had to be done. His tone, consequently, could be highly disparaging:

It is to be feared that many moral agencies do little more than tamper with the symptoms of our social maladies. Intoxication, idleness, irreligion, and crime, are too often treated as primary, instead of secondary causes, or solely effects; but are they not the legitimate consequences of the want of sound education and early moral training, irregular employment, unwholesome dwellings, and utter absence of rational recreations for the victims of these terrible evils? Even the Temperance Movement, which is doing so much good in reducing the drinking customs of the upper and middle classes, does not fulfil its mission. Root out the drunkard! He still springs up, and ever will while the circumstances that produce him remain. Ireland, Scotland, the neglected classes of our own country illustrate these assertions.[4]

Employment, Poverty and Charity

Dare's *Reports* contain regular references to the economic and employment situation in Leicester. The period was characterized by continual ups and downs in trade, under-employment in the town's staple hosiery industry being a noticeable feature throughout. Critical of *laissez-faire* economics, Dare argued, in 1852, that partial and irregular employment was:

the primary source of all the evils that afflict the working classes. Want of regular employment induces idleness, involuntary no doubt in the beginning, but confirmed in many instances by repetition. Habits are contracted that too often torment the whole of after-existence. Ignorance, drunkenness, brutal crimes, beggary, enlistment, felony - these are the frightful progeny of slack seasons. Labour is all working men as a body want. Charity they do not want. That human beings should suffer because "doll's eyes" may have grown dull in the market, is a social morbidity that our State-physicians will do well to remove.[1]

The point is underlined in Dare's *Report* for 1858, when he presents a detailed account of the hardships experienced by the working classes during a particularly depressed period:

The past winter was one of the most trying and difficult that I have ever experienced. My door was literally besieged with clamorous suppliants, greatly increased, no doubt, by the injudicious conduct of certain public, and professedly religious speakers, who, desirous of popularity, shun no means for its attainment. In imitation of parties at Preston, Nottingham, and other places, where great distress was experienced, they began their agitation here before it had really commenced. A room was opened for the record of names as requisitionists to the Mayor and the Guardians of the poor. About fifteen hundred signatures were obtained, but nearly half of the persons that signed were unmarried, thus showing that the agitation had called out chiefly the reckless and undeserving. The movement greatly increased the difficulties of the season by assuming a somewhat threatening aspect and by raising expectations that could not be realised. To this cause also, in some measure, may the unusual number of persons begging from house to house be attributed.

Inflamed by agitation, and dragged from their homes to the pasture, to the recreation ground, or the Market-place, to listen to violent addresses, they naturally resorted to begging by way of finishing up their public efforts. It is sad when in times of political excitement, the self-interested prey upon the unthinking, but it is still more sad when in commercial depressions the religious functionary aims at applause by means that strike at the very roots of law and order. Another marked feature of the season was the number of very little children sent out to beg, some with a bag, others with a basket tied to their neck. It is to be feared that many of these sent out so early to beg will acquire the habit for life. Talking on this subject to a working man, he observed, "It used to be strangers who came a begging, but now it is our own neighbours and people whom we know." As the winter wore on distress became very general, and the working classes suffered great privation; the double house was given up for the single one; in many streets numbers of dwellings became empty whose families crowded with others into abodes already occupied, for the sake of lessening their rent. The small means which the more careful had laid up, whether in money, clothing, or furniture, were applied for daily wants, till the house looked desolate and the inmates were left without a change of apparel, or anything worthy of the name of bed-clothing. Numbers struggled for a long time in this manner, till forced at last by sheer hunger into the Union house. I called one day on a well known family, who live in a row of several houses. Their little girl was just recovering from fever, and she wished for an orange, but her mother hadn't a halfpenny to buy one, nor could she borrow so much in the whole row. Another family had saved by great care upwards of twelve pounds, with the hope of keeping it for sickness or old age, but this was slowly applied for "daily bread," till the whole was consumed, having had no work for more than six months. One day a young woman obtained from me a dispensary ticket for her brother who was suffering from consumption, and whose death was finally hastened by privation. I found from her conversation that the greater part of the family had been driven into the Union house by starvation.

Leicester workhouse - later Hillcrest Hospital - in the 1870s, with the staff outside. The last 'refuge' for the destitute

Working-class collective self-help: the founders of the Leicester Coop Society in 1860. Left to right: J. Woodford, G. Sharpe, G. Herbert, T. Norton (Sec.), S. Wilford, H.C. Burrows, E. Silverwood

She herself objected to go in because of the mixed company and disreputable characters that are placed together without classification. She had therefore pledged all her best clothes to purchase food, and a few days before, in the depth of winter, she said she had pulled off her flannel petticoat to pawn for a loaf of bread; the consequence was that she took a violent cold and was ill for many weeks. How sad, that young girls should be reduced to such straits, and there were numbers in a similar position during the winter! There can be little doubt that sheer want is one chief cause of increasing what has been politely termed "the great social evil" of the age. Numbers driven from home by necessity went in little gangs of six or eight on begging excursions, and roamed hundreds of miles. They stay out for a month or five weeks at a time, and send home what little sums they may obtain beyond their own support. An individual of one of these parties, a respectable working man, whom I have known for a long period, who frequently attends our evening worship, and who would by no means beg in his native town, informed me that in their last excursion they took a round that included Melton, Grantham, Newark, Southwell, Lincoln, Louth, Pontefract, York, Doncaster, Leeds, Macclesfield, Derby, &c., and so back to Leicester. They walk from twenty to thirty miles a day, "calling" the places through which they pass. In some instances, after stating their condition, the Mayor would give them leave to "sing and beg" in his locality. Musical parties succeed the best, especially if they can manage a few catches or glees; persons will often listen to "the vocal air" when deaf to the voice of supplication.

I find that in all my monthly reports, from September till after Whitsuntide, references are made to a similar condition of things. The constant cry in my visits was "We have no work; nothing to do; if we could but get some work, the parish will not help us; they will only give an order." Hence, for the greater part of the year, visiting was a very trying and painful duty. It was indeed very painful to call time after time upon well known families who from long failure of employment had exhausted all their means, and upon whom hunger was pressing. Though there was no public subscription for the relief of the necessitous, I believe there was much done to soften their sufferings by private benevolence, assisted by the kindly co-operation of the Mayor, who, during his two very difficult years of office, manifested on all occasions a christian sympathy for the poor.

As might be expected, the long continuance of distress furnished a plea for much imposture in begging, some of which was concocted and carried out under a regularly organised system. There was in the town a party of practised beggars, who formed a committee among themselves, that held its regular sittings to fabricate tales of distress, and draw up begging papers. Then a certain number were despatched with them to victimise the credulous, and at the end of the day they all assembled to share up their booty and enjoy themselves in "feasting and riotous living;" very little, if any of the proceeds, being taken to their families. The parties acting in this disreputable manner belong to the town, but as I know them all, they have long since ceased their attempts at imposition upon myself. From being so central there are always a great many mendicants passing through the town, and I have again detected several shameless fabrications. Amongst other cases I would strongly caution against parties soliciting money for funerals instead of letting them be defrayed by the parish. None should be assisted without inquiry, as charity in these cases is often abused, very unnecessary expense is incurred, and too frequently the gatherings of mourners terminate in a drunken revel. I know a case where the grandmother of a deceased child gave orders "for a first-rate coffin and furniture," while the mother of the dead little one was out begging for money to bury it, with a companion who was to have part of the proceeds for helping her beg and showing her where to go. In another similar case, two women volunteered to beg for the burial of a deceased neighbour, but they kept back a portion of the money, and in a third case the collectors were observed "under a dark wall" appropriating a part of the contributions they had obtained, just before giving an account of them to the relatives of the deceased. But even in these cases there are exceptions, and a little kindly assistance is deserved and gratefully received.

Some of the most distressing cases I met with were those of poor women during, and just after confinement. Reduced by low and insufficient diet, they almost sunk under the additional burden. In several of these cases, the tickets kindly forwarded by Mr. Mott, allowing the holders to go for a pint of ale or porter for seven successive days were of great service. A portion of the tickets also were for wine, which imparted much comfort to others during sickness....

There is at all times amongst the aged, and less skilful, and those occupied in trades, falling into desuetude, through invention and improved machinery, a great difficulty to obtain a living, and in seasons like the past they suffer greatly; but I bear cheerful testimony to the patient and manly manner in which all classes endured their privations, still hoping for better times, and which is fully corroborated by Mr. Stone the Town Clerk's able report. Still it is much to be lamented, that, with the certain knowledge of the almost regular recurrence of commercial depressions, the working classes, as a body, make little or no provision for them. In seasons of prosperity they forget that hardest of all duties - present sacrifice for future benefit. Absorbed wholly in the passing moment, while the tide flows,

"They ape the follies of the great,
They curse the burdens of the state,
Yet greater for themselves create,
By reckless waste and crime.
Whate'er's a foot, abroad, at home,
The pipe must blaze, the tankard foam,
And circus, fair, and farce consume,
Saint Monday's loss of time."

One of the greatest blessings that could be conferred on the working man, would be regular occupation from day to day, and not by "fits and starts." Excessive toil at one time, and enforced idleness at another, are alike destructive of social and moral improvement. Both produce exhaustion which creates a morbid craving for stimulants, and long privation often begets exasperation of mind and indifference to the spiritual life. The body reduced by physical want, falls a prey to disease. Children become shoeless, adults become without change of clothing, the Sunday school is neglected, the house of God deserted, and tribulation is borne rather with the feelings of the stoic, than in the spirit of the blessed Redeemer, "who had not where to lay his head."[2]

In 1868, Dare noted how even the more respectable working classes, like the better-paid workers in the 'fancy' branches of the hosiery trade, were subjected to long annual periods of economic privation, and that this could set them on a downward moral course:

The Savings Bank, Grey Friars, 1870s. Dare hoped the bank would encourage working-class thrift

I have intimated that the year has been a difficult period to some of the workers. I find from my monthly reports that the winter opened with snow early in December, and though the weather generally was not so cold as some winters, yet we had a great deal of what some people called "miserable weather." Rain, day after day, till every scene and every object grew chill and cheerless. Provisions of all kinds were excessively dear and employment in many branches either very partial or altogether suspended. For instance, the fancy branches are subject to long depressions. Improved machinery and various other causes seem to be superseding or altering the modes of production in this branch. During such transitions of industrial appliances there is necessarily much privation. I know several of this class who have had to struggle a long time against this untoward combination of circumstances. And as the persons engaged in these tasteful fabrics are for the most part the more intelligent of the workers, they feel

Framework knitters in a local workshop, c.1880

their privations the more keenly. Six, eight, ten weeks, or even several months every year they are without "any work to do." These suspensions of adult labour lead to the sad necessity of parents pressing on their children for means to carry on the household. Hence, even from this class originates a downward tendency. The children soon know their earnings support the family; that the parents are dependent, so they quickly break from all restraint, and untaught and untrained, assume the airs of grown-up people.[3]

'Change of social conditions,' Dare argued in 1859, 'always causes a change of moral manifestations.' Prosperous years, of course, brought about 'a more cheerful tone' amongst the working classes.[4] Dare was particularly optimistic in his view of working-class life in 1853, during a notably sound economic period:

Looking back over the whole year, it has been, as regards employment and wages, a time of unusual prosperity. Till the recent rise in various articles of consumption, the working classes generally were never so well off, nor evinced so much cheerfulness and gratitude since I have laboured amongst them. I feel I can safely assert that among many of them a much better tone of feeling and improved habits prevail. An increasing desire for knowledge is widely manifested. Unbelief is tempered with more candor and liberality, and social subjects approached with a deeper sense of the importance of self-government. They have a higher relish for more rational amusements and a better reading taste. Excursion trains, rural fêtes, social meetings, and tea gatherings, with music and recitations, have been more frequent and generally speaking well conducted. Mr. Nicholson informs me of the pleasing fact, that no policeman was called in amongst the twenty-five thousand who visited his promenade concerts on the Cricket Ground, and the holidays spent in the country are no longer characterised by drunkenness and brutality. No doubt a softening influence has been produced by many of the employers and their friends mingling with "the hands" in their summer festivities.[5]

During depressed periods of employment and trade, Dare considered - often very briefly unfortunately - a number of ways in which working-class poverty and distress was, and might be further, alleviated. He regularly referred, for instance, to the way many of the working classes assisted one another by clubbing together whatever meagre means they possessed.[6] He noted in 1856 how many:

subsisted on the roots from their little gardens, for days together; others went into the fields to gather haws, which they sold to raise quick from, at eightpence per strike, and thus, from day to day, obtained a morsel of food.[7]

In the same year, Dare also referred to 'some employers' who had kept their establishments open during the depressed period in order to mitigate the widespread distress.[8]

In 1861, he drew attention to many little working-class shops that were springing up during the depression, selling a few meagre vegetables, sweetmeats and other trifling articles that could 'really afford no more support than drowning men secure by clutching at straws'.[9]

Dare persistently demanded wider employment opportunities for the town's working classes. He was in favour of the growth of factories, regarding factory workers as better paid and having better working conditions.[10] He often drew attention to the number of new warehouses and workshops being built, and in 1862 he commended the arrival of new trades in Leicester:

Hodges and Sons' elastic-web factory on Welford Road, 1870s. The elastic-web industry expanded in the town in the period. It was mainly factory-based

Referring to trade and means of employment, several fresh branches of industry have been lately introduced. Within a few years the elastic fabrics; improved fancy hosiery of very beautiful descriptions; together with clog-making and the newly-invented shoe trades have greatly increased the material prosperity of the town, and happily preserved it from the fearful privations of the northern counties.[11]

Even with the arrival of these new trades, however, it seemed clear to Dare that, amongst certain workers, there was:

little aptitude and less inclination to turn to any other pursuit than that they have followed. The idea of changing their occupation is disliked; use, to them, is more than second nature. There is also an objection amongst employers to setting on unaccustomed hands.[12]

One important criticism which Dare lodged over the way the local community catered for the needs of the poor during depressed times, was that against the local Board of Guardians for their policy of rigidly adhering to the letter of the 1834 Poor Law. In 1862, for instance:

The greater portion of the past year was marked with scarcity of employment and consequent privation and sickness. There appears to be annually a flat interval from December to the opening of spring, during which period my door is almost daily thronged with applicants for advice or relief. Their distress arises chiefly from the want of employment. As soon as this fails, all the poorer kinds of workmen are thrown immediately into necessitous circumstances, and commence their old course of appealing to private alms-giving. No doubt they suffer a great deal, yet it is not right, except in peculiar cases, that they should seek assistance from private benevolence. Nor can it be quite right that nothing but the everlasting order should be offered by the relieving officer. The honest poor man, whose love of independence deters him from applying for relief till all other means have failed, seems to require in seasons of depression some kind of outdoor labour, not of a degrading, but if possible, remunerative character, otherwise our admirable poor-law machinery breaks down and turns the poor into paupers or beggars. Its chief boast of efficiency is "So many rates saved," "So many less in the house," "So many more have refused the order", not "Is there less real want amongst the poor?" "Is there less suffering and sickness?" "Is there less crime and fewer beggars in the land?" It is to be feared that the present mode of administering the poor-laws tends to increase mendicancy, and greatly adds throughout the country to the number of the common lodging-houses - those dens of crime and infamy.[13]

A boy queueing at a Leicester public soup kitchen, 1870s

During times of widespread unemployment and poverty, Dare advocated the setting up of public charities such as soup kitchens.[14] In addition, he argued the case for private charity as a means of softening the temporary afflictions of the unfortunate, deserving poor, in order to tide them over their temporary difficulties and to preserve them from what he termed the 'degradation of parish pay'.[15] At the same time,

Common lodging-house on Green Street. Dare regarded the residents of such places as the most disreputable of the working classes

however, he argued strongly against indiscriminate alms-giving on the grounds that it encouraged dependency and professional mendicancy. His argument is well put in 1855:

The present year, as a whole, has been a period of much difficulty and privation. The winter was long and of unusual severity; employment was partial, till the return of the harvest; fuel and provisions very dear. As all articles of consumption still continue high, and the staple branches are, I understand, chiefly occupied in completing orders for the war, considerable apprehension prevails lest the returning winter should add to the privations of the last two years. Should these fears be unhappily realised, I should earnestly recommend the opening of two or three public soup kitchens, as none then, especially poor children, need suffer hunger, as numbers did last winter. Besides, this mode of relief is a good protection against imposture; it cannot be abused as the gift in money from private benevolence.

Unless temporary pressures are met by some provision of this kind, a spirit of beggary is often awakened by private charity, and the habit implanted for life in many who would never have begged at all, had their passing distress been thus relieved. I know personally that much evil was done last winter by indiscriminate giving at the door. A benevolent, but inexperienced, person stated that he had given eight or ten sixpences daily for some time to parties calling at the door, and that they chiefly came from B-. Street, and neighbourhood. Now nearly the whole of these would consist of Irish, and our less reputable poor - parties who will not submit to the regulations of the Union House, but who above all should be relieved in no other way. These make a harvest of bad times, while the deserving who shun alike begging and the work-house, pine in silence and want. The majority of begging cases come from the common lodging houses and the resident Irish. Except in extreme cases, these latter are not allowed, and very properly, any out-door relief; for the smallest out-door allowance would be an inducement for the recipients to send for their relations by the hundred to come and share their good fortune. But they will not submit to the necessary regulations of the Union House, so they have recourse to mendicancy. They are encouraged to pursue this course by their faith, being perpetually told that before the institution of the poor-laws, the church took care of the necessitous, and would again, if her rightful possessions were restored, so they follow begging without shame, as their just inheritance, not knowing that in the "good old times," hundreds of their class were hung yearly, "as rogues and vagabonds."

Much care is required in bestowing assistance, lest a feeling of dependence, or a hypocritical pretence of religion be generated. I have known families, part of whom have attended one place of worship, and part another, with a view of obtaining gifts of charity from both. Alms-giving, as a primary means of removing social distress, is a fallacious idea. "Benevolences" should lead to self-help and self-reliance, or they are an evil. Age, sickness, accident, exigency, claim our sympathy, but even here discrimination is required. I give to none with whom I am not acquainted, or of whom I cannot obtain reliable information. All lodging-house cases should, without exception, be referred to the relieving officer. During the winter, as may be readily imagined, I met with many objects of real compassion. Numbers, disliking to break up their homes for the Union, or to clamour for charity at private houses, suffered in silence both cold and hunger, their Sunday clothes, and all other available articles being pledged for the bread that perisheth. Amidst so much privation, disease, and consequent mortality, it is necessary to exhibit practical proofs of our sympathy, and give a meaning to the words - "be ye warmed, be ye clothed, be ye fed."[16]

Dare regularly condemned the practices of professional beggars. In 1854, for instance:

Parents even are depraved as to make the afflictions of their offspring the means of a livelihood. A short time ago I inquired into a case where an idiotic child was carried from door to door to excite charity upon which the whole family, two parents and three children -

subsisted. They had strolled from Bedfordshire to this town, and so they pass from place to place, taking up their temporary abode either in the ready furnished pest hole, or the common lodging house. The former of these places, under a certain rental, should be licensed as the latter are. An important moral and sanitary improvement might be effected if all these sort of "lodgings for travellers" could be consolidated in one public building and placed under regular inspection. But the two worst cases were amongst the Irish. Two or three Irish children were observed by a benevolent lady on the race-course the Sunday before last; these children were in such a "ragged filthy condition as to be a disgrace to a christian country. Could anything be done for them?" I made inquiries of a respectable neighbour whom I have known for twenty years, and who has known these same Irish families four or five years. The mother of two of the said children lives in that respectable locality, "Pork-shop Yard." She has offspring by several men - is "enceinte" and perpetually drunk. She sends out her children in this condition on purpose to excite commiseration; if the children were dressed up tidy to-day, the clothes would all be stripped off, sold for drink, and the children driven forth half naked to play the same game tomorrow. The other Irish case is that of a man, a widower, who shortened his wife's existence by ill-treatment. He lives, himself, by gathering rags and bones and begging. He takes no care whatever of his children. They are sent at large in rags and dirt to obtain subsistence in any manner they are able. A better garment or a pair of shoes would be immediately taken from them for drink: the boy seen on the race-course was recently in prison for theft. Should not the Irish generally be referred to their own priest? They are a great calamity to our large towns. Wherever they locate they introduce crime, disease, and wretchedness. There is scarcely an Irish case deserving of relief. The police should have orders to clear the public walks and race-course, especially on a Sunday of all such objects as referred to above. They are sent there for the express purpose of preying on the unwary. Some idea may be formed of the low cunning of the Irish from the following fact which came under the notice of my informant, who keeps a wood yard, and often supplies these people with wood which they split up for sale in small quantities. An Irishman, one day, came for a certain quantity of wood for which he wanted trust. He tried every art of persuasion, stating how much it would accommodate him - how he should be dammed without - how he was foodless and penniless, &c., &c., - but as the wood merchant was inexorable, and he found if no money there would be no wood, he asked "if the mistress could lend him just a pair of scissors?" The scissors being produced he proceeded to take off his waistcoat and then carefully opened a pipe like formation in the inside of the back of the garment. From this secret hoard he produced from four others a sovereign to pay for the wood. On being remonstrated with, for telling such an hypocritical tale, he merely replied he didn't want to "disturb the craters," and he could soon have turned the wood into money that should have paid for it. And thus there is no believing any of their statements.

Professional beggars injure the deserving poor, by swallowing up the means of private charity, and discouraging the kind hearted by their profligacy and lies.[17]

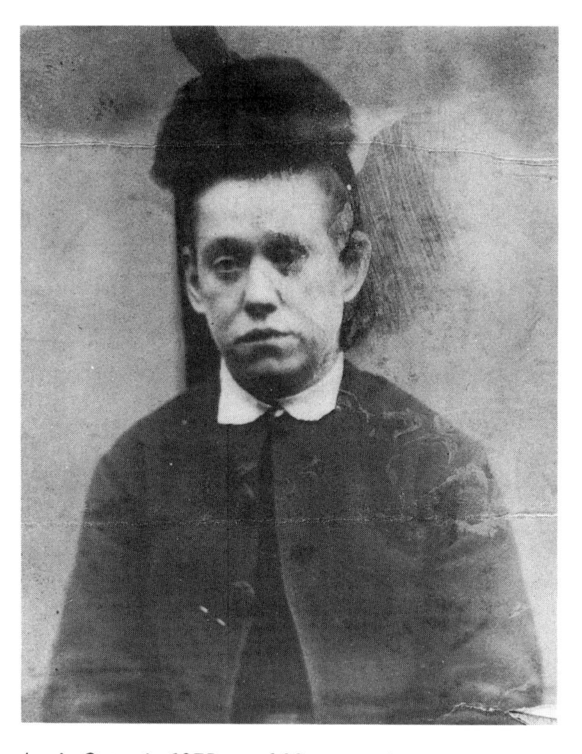

Annie Orton in 1875, aged 22, a prostitute

In his references to professional mendicancy, Dare drew a distinction between resident beggars and the wandering vagrants of common lodging-houses. The latter were worse by far in his view. They operated in gangs and practised particularly ingenious ploys. Some lodging-house keepers evidently supplied them - 'at a fixed charge' - with lists of known, gullible, benevolent people in the area for them to work on.[18] In 1855 Dare described in detail the stock fabrications employed by different grades of strolling beggars:

It will be remembered that recently a Judge of this circuit made some very heavy charges as to the criminal condition of Leicester, characterising it as marked above other places for crime. As one of its moral agents moving for the last ten years amongst its most neglected classes, and having visited in annual conferences, many other principal places, I felt these unqualified censures to be unjust. They were, in fact, a

Pawnbrokers like Whyall's on Humberstone Road played a vital role in working-class economy

gratuitous reflection, not only upon our less fortunate fellow-creatures, but also upon the many noble and christian efforts in operation for their physical improvement and moral elevation. I therefore obtained the criminal statistics from six other large towns, intending to give in this Report a digest of the crime in such places as Birmingham, Derby, and Newcastle, compared with that of Leicester. But this I find would occupy more space than can be allowed for the whole report; or it might easily be shown, that though there is much to deplore, this town is not worse in its criminal condition, if so bad, as many other places. This is certainly not very satisfactory, but it proves that the causes of crime are widely spread, and till these are removed, as already intimated, their effects will be similar, in similar populations all over the country.

Our esteemed and learned Recorder, in a recent address, rightly urged the prevention of crime by education and early religious training. From inquiries I have no doubt that much of the undetected crime is committed by the wandering inmates of the common lodging houses. From information obligingly furnished by Mr. Goodyer, superintendent of the county police, I find that there are about seventy thousand lodgings annually supplied to these kind of vagrants in this county alone. That gentleman also states that these seventy thousand lodgings will represent about two thirds of that number as separate individuals. So that there are about fifty thousand vagrants passing every year through this county, the majority of whom are obtaining their subsistence by very questionable means. It appears probable, from the following return kindly supplied by Serjeant Wright, Inspector of Nuisances, that about half this number of "wandering individuals" pass through the Borough of Leicester, as he states: "There are in Leicester thirty-eight common lodging-houses registered; these are registered to accommodate,

Nightly 587 persons
Weekly 4109 "
Yearly 213668 "

The above includes the families of the keepers of the lodging houses."

These facts unfold a sad feature in our social condition as the greater number of those who frequent the common lodging houses obtain their subsistence by preying on the public. Scarcely one of them pursues any honest means of living, though each has what may be called his professional method of gulling the unwary. A lodging-house keeper, whom I formerly knew in very different circumstances, informed me of the following tricks practised by parties who had lodged at his house. I copy them with the hope of checking imposture. As in every other fraternity, there are grades even in vagrancy, and parties are named according to the line of swindling they adopt. The first class of beggars are called "High-Flyers." These are generally shrewd, quick-witted fellows, who have received some education. They go well dressed; they can draw up a petition or begging letter, and are never at a loss for some plausible fabrication. On coming into a new locality they inquire of the lodging-house keeper, or of his lodgers, respecting the names and character of all who are likely to answer their designs. The High-flyer then makes his applications stating to his victims that their fathers, or some branch of the family, were on visiting terms; that he knows some of their relatives, whom he takes care to name, together with the minister or magistrate of the neighbourhood; they have all been intimate with his family; since he has been reduced they had been very kind to him, is now in the last extremity; wants the means to get home, or has heard of some good situation if he could obtain clothes and a little cash to enter upon it, &c., &c. If my informant spoke truly, a gentleman on the London Road recently gave one of this fraternity a sovereign; if less than gold is presented they think the application has failed. "Forney-Squarers" are another class; these make finger rings out of brass buttons; they use large coat buttons; they stamp two rings out of each button; they have a complete set of tools, such as stamps, delicate hammers, files, brushes, wash-leathers, paste for polishing, &c; they make the rings look quite eyeable; they go with them amongst servants, or "the slavies" as they call them, and make from two to four shillings for each of the rings. But they do not refuse even sixpence for a ring if they can get a "good cant" with it. A "cant" consists of bread, cheese, butter, meat, tea, sugar, flour, or any article of clothing. They bring home as much as half a stone of flour, half a loaf, a pound of bacon, at a time, and other articles in proportion, in exchange for these brass rings. The men make these rings at their

'Spring-heel Jack' - real name John Preston: a street-hawker from the period

lodgings, and send out their female companions to dispose of them. They do not take many out at once for fear of the police. They generally wear a couple on their fingers, and put one or two in their bosoms; they often take a spurious brooch or two as well, which they procure at the "swag-shops," as they term toy establishments. Of course they always pretend to be forced to sell these articles through great distress - having a sick child or husband, or some relative lying dead, &c.

Another class are called "China-Fakers;" these profess to be menders of broken articles of china or glass; they sometimes join this to the previous branch, the wife or daughter trafficking in "gold," while the man looks after the china, &c. "These always," says my informant, "get plenty - from five to fifteen shillings per day, and after their rounds have beef-steaks, toast, eggs, and whatever else they fancy."

"Driss-Fencers," or, rather, I suppose, dress-fencers, are those who foist spurious lace on unsuspecting ladies. They first purchase a quantity of the commonest lace, and then prepare it by putting it into a bag containing some yellow sand; they "swing it backwards and forwards in all directions," which imparts to the lace a rich golden colour, and a thread-like appearance; it is then well shaken and ironed. This they hawk as pillow-lace, which they have just finished, and are obliged to sell at a great loss through some sad misfortune; the price is varied according to the gullibility of the customer. My informant stated that he has had persons prepare lace in this manner at his house, and that he has known them to get from two shillings to ten or twelve shillings per day by selling it; at night the money is squandered in waste and profligacy. Another trick which they practise is called "The Widow's Lurk." A female obtains a widow's cap and other suitable apparel - she may have a husband living, or never been married - she borrows a child or two, if she have none of her own, and thus begs from door to door, with some lamentable tale of bereavement. The same informant told me, he had known one woman in particular, who regularly went on this errand, while her husband lived in idleness, playing at cards, and smoking and drinking in the lodging-house day after day. And if at night she did not bring enough home he would beat his "widow" for her ill luck. Sometimes in the evening these mock widows stand in some conspicuous place or sit on the step of a door to excite charity; this they call "standing pad." By these hypocritical means they obtain sufficient to live on the choicest food, and keep their husbands without using any means towards a living. "Griddlers," or, "Chanters," are the ballad singers who drawl out miserable tunes, set to some terrible mishap which has befallen them. The "Griddler" takes a "Mumper" with him, who holds the hat, or begs from door to door, while the "Chanter" doles out his ditty. "Paste-lurkers" hawk a composition for cleaning brass, tin, and pewter articles. They obtain a bath-brick, value twopence, a farthing's worth of raddle, a few pounds of whitening, and a small quantity of turpentine; with these ingredients they make about eight shillings worth of polishing paste to brighten up the public. Some of the inmates of the lodging-houses do not seem to possess sufficient genius to follow any of these mysteries of the craft, but pursue begging only; these are said to go on the "Down Right," or "Monkery," as they term it. These various classes are continually shifting their quarters; they stay about a month or six weeks in one locality; they then decamp to another, making a certain round, in nearly a given time. Some of them visit Melton, Oakham, Uppingham, Market Harborough, Lutterworth, Hinckley, touching at all the intermediate villages, and then back to Leicester. Others take Loughborough, Nottingham, Derby, Burton, Ashby, Atherstone, Nuneaton, Hinckley, with adjacent villages, and so back to this town. Most of the men have a partner, married or otherwise; some of them undertake the out door business, while the women remain in the lodging-houses; others turn them out to beg, &c., while they themselves remain at home in utter idleness. When talking amongst themselves they cannot be understood by the uninitiated.

"Timber Merchants." These, chiefly Irish, split wood for sale and hawk it from door to door. The children sent to sell it are designedly turned out shoeless and in rags to secure purchasers or charity; they are tasked as to the quantity they must sell; if possible they are a

worse description of beggars than the classes already enumerated.

Thus we have in "our midst" an organised system of vice and beggary, supported by the unthinking and pseudo-benevolent. It will never be eradicated till people cease relieving without inquiry and public lodging-houses are substituted for the present private ones.[19]

The misappropriation of medical charity-tickets was evidently a particular ploy used by Leicester's resident beggars as well as by the strollers:

Like the strolling frequenters of the lodging houses, our resident beggars seem to have their stock fabrications. One, lately practised on a benevolent lady, is to pretend that a relative is ill, dangerously ill, and going into the Infirmary. An in-patient ticket has been secured, but "a change of linen and flannel is absolutely necessary, and must be provided, or the patient will not be admitted. A shirt, whether linen or flannel, or some little help towards purchasing either would be so useful, and so kindly bestowed." Now it is ten to one that such an appeal is an utter falsehood. There is no sick relative, and the garments if bestowed would be immediately pawned or made away with for drink. On investigation, I found a second case of this kind a bare-faced fabrication. Another plan is to have a bandaged limb, and profess to be an out-patient at the Infirmary. Such statement was made to a kind lady who wished me to examine the case. I wrote to the man's last employer, as he said, in Wales. The letter was quickly sent back, through the "dead letter office," marked "insufficient address." On going to inquire further, I found the man had decamped, and thus my suspicions were confirmed. The plan he pursued is an old trick. On coming to a fresh place, a ticket is procured from some well meaning but unreflecting person, for some medical institution. The patient feigns sickness, or a diseased limb, the latter is most convenient. The applicant has plenty of work as soon as he is fit to go to it. Has been a patient so long; the doctor says he must rest; will soon be better with the treatment; never in the habit of begging - is ashamed of it, hates it; longs to get to work again, - hopes therefore to obtain a little help till he can resume his usual employment. I believe one inquiry among beggars is whether there be an Infirmary in such and such a place, and the fact, whether there is or not determines the direction of their journey. At any rate this plan is a stock piece with beggars, and it shows how careful persons should be in the bestowal of tickets. Like other kinds of relief, none should be given to parties whose characters are unknown. A fourth case was a man begging for an elastic knee cap. It would only cost fifteen shillings. He could then get to work. I found that this was an

Alfred Simpson in 1872, aged 32; sentenced to 7 years' imprisonment for stealing linen

habitual stroller. I had seen him on a previous occasion. After victimising several kind ladies in this town he decamped, and was apprehended in a neighbouring town for practising the same imposition.[20]

Dare accordingly demanded caution in the distribution of medical charity-tickets. In addition, he felt that the opening of the new Dispensary in 1866 would do much to:

annihilate misapplied charity. It speaks well for the prudence and self-respect of the workers that upwards of 5000 have become members, and thus secured themselves from the need of charity tickets and parish doctors. As the benefits are available on such reasonable terms, it becomes a question whether free tickets should not be witheld, for, judging from the circumstances and characters of those who have applied to me for them, it is only the improvident, or nearly so, who rely upon them, instead of making the small self-sacrifice in the time of health that would secure all the privileges of membership. Of course, there are exceptions, but as these would be personally known to honorary subscribers or their almoners, such cases might be met by direct purchase of free tickets. For similar reasons it requires very great care in bestowing both the in-patient and out-patient tickets of the Infirmary, especially as the funds of that excellent institution are inadequate to its requirements. Indeed, I have long thought that it would be very advisable to adopt the self-supporting principle, if only in a limited degree, at the Infirmary. It would tend, in some measure, to check careless habits and dependency. As long as there is a chance of obtaining free tickets, many will make no provision for sickness. Besides, the adoption of this principle would add to the funds. I find, from the report of the Infirmary for the last year, that 4,674 out-patient tickets were presented, besides those admitted as "accidents," or "emergencies," making the number of out-patients for the year, 6,351. Throwing out the accidents and emergencies, though I do not see why they should not be reckoned, the average number of out-patient tickets will be from four to five thousand; but say four thousand, and the average number of in-patient tickets one thousand, though these numbers are far below the mark. Now, if the out-patients on presenting their tickets were to pay 6d. each, and the in-patients 1s. each on theirs, the funds would be annually increased £150. This plan would force applicants to make some little self-sacrifice, and teach them to reflect that this noble institution has to be supported by the voluntary contributions of the benevolent. The "hands" in all factories, warehouses, and shops should forward their gatherings to its funds.[21]

Dare was also critical of charity being provided by political or religious groups as a means of furthering their particular causes and ambitions:

There is a vast amount of destitution and suffering amongst certain classes, which, in our present social and political condition, it is impossible wholly to remove; in fact, it can only be mitigated. And yet, in reference to these classes, are not our public charities, to say nothing of private benevolence, exercised rather with a view to serve the purposes of sect and party, than to soften distress as such? "Where do you send your children to school - what place of worship do you attend?" is always asked with marked significance before the bands of charity are unbound, which shows too plainly that it is not of that kind which "hopeth and beareth all things."[22]

Increasingly in the period Dare detected a more determined resolution in the town to curb indiscriminate charity and to suppress both begging and vagrancy. In 1872, he presents a particularly optimistic picture, at the same time arguing the case for a more systematic administration of local charity:

From accounts obtained at the County Office and from the Board of Guardians, it is also very satisfactory to find that vagrancy has greatly diminished during the past year. There have been fewer wayfarers or persons pretending to be in search of work; fewer vagrants in the lodging-houses, and fewer tramps seeking relief. An intelligent officer attributes this improvement partly to the great call for labour and increased wages; but chiefly to the decrease of indiscriminate charity, whereby the mendicant finds his "occupation gone." This is the true secret of his disappearance. So long as ill-directed benevolence makes it more profitable for him to beg than to work, so long will he infest the country. Let there be no idle alms-giving, and then there will be no idle vagabonds scattering their filth, and disease, and obscenity over the land. There are always plenty of well known deserving objects to call forth our kindest sympathy: these, after due inquiry, should be assisted.

The time has fully arrived when all kinds of charity should be organized and systematically administered. Without constant vigilance public charities only foster a spirit of dependency. It is very doubtful whether the "Blanket-lending Society," the "Ladies Lying-in Society," and even the "Sutton Charity," do not fall into this category. Parties who have once obtained blankets or the bag, never think of doing without them; indeed, they feel injured if refused. It would be an improvement if these institutions took somewhat the form of benefit societies, the recipients raising by small subscriptions the means of carrying them on. Many a mean fellow designedly deserts his poor wife during her confinement, well-knowing that his "guardian angels," as he calls them, will come forward to supply the poor creature's wants. Were it possible, the "Sutton Charity" would more nearly realize the benevolent and truly christian designs of its founder, if it could be applied in the form of a Sanatorium, like that recently opened in London by the Lord Mayor, Sir Sidney Waterlow, or the one at Alton Towers and other parts of the country, as at Huddersfield by the late C. Brookes, Esq., of Enderby, where the convalescent might be fully restored by proper diet, repose, and fresh air. At present, in many cases the money bestowed on dismissal from the Infirmary is laid out in showy articles of dress, or wasted in hurtful stimulants; and even where invalids are wishful to apply properly the largess, the attempt, before full recovery, to resume their labours, often ends in fatal relapse. No one should fill up the applicant's papers without full knowledge of the individual. In passing, I would again repeat let all charities be speedily organized, with a strong infusion of lay agency. Past governments have increased vagabondism, by dismissing crippled soldiers and sailors and Waterloo heroes without pensions, and sending them to beg through the kingdom, to show how they estimate the services of the noble fellows who have "fought for their King and country." These and their families should be cared for by the government, and their pitiable fellow-vagrants, who have been disabled in dangerous occupations, should be supported from some common funds levied by employers; at any rate, vagrancy must be suppressed.[23]

Environment and Health

Dare contended throughout his *Reports* that there was a causal relationship between physical environment, health and behaviour. In 1846, for instance:

Few can form a just estimation of the difficulties with which the poor have to contend, in the labour of self-improvement. The listless indifference and hopeless passiveness engendered by a continual inadequacy of physical comforts, shut out self-respect; and the cares of the present swallow up all thoughts of the future life. The animal is not properly provided for, therefore, the mind is neglected; the body pines, and the spirit languishes. Some idea of the difficulty of the task may be formed from the following circumstances that recently came under my observation. One little girl was kept away from school the Sunday before last because her mother was in a state of intoxication the whole of the day. She pawned every article of clothing in the house; her sons sat without their shirts, and all of them were without food. In this house, which consists of an up and down-stairs room, live six or seven persons; a man, unmarried to the mother, who is a widow, sleeps on the chairs; and the bed, the only one in the house, is occupied by the mother, a grown-up daughter, the little girl referred to above, and two sons, one eleven or twelve, and the other fifteen or sixteen years of age. Two other little girls were absent on the same Sunday. On enquiring the cause, I found their mother was confined on that day; her husband deserted her some years ago; consequently this addition to her family and her burdens is illegitimate, beside the shocking example set to her own children. What can counteract such immoral influences? Yet these are the ulcers, that require probing to the bottom, and rooting out of the social system, before it can be restored to perfect sanity.[1]

The problem of just keeping warm made domestic decency difficult, as Dare noted in 1847:

I have found too little bed-clothing in poor families a great evil. There is no doubt that this leads directly to the demoralizing practice of so many huddling together in sleep; they do so for the sake of warmth. I visited a family, consisting of the parents and three children, where there was but one up-stairs room, and but one wretched bed. The eldest was a daughter about fifteen years of age. They all slept together, and the mother was recently confined. Another family, with four children, was exactly in the same situation. The children slept at the bottom of the bed, or feet to feet with the parents. One old man told me, with the utmost naïveté, that he thus "used his boy all the winter to keep his feet warm instead of a bottle of hot water," or the cold would have killed him. I believe there was but one pair of blankets - and those from the society - among these families. Numbers of large families are thus situated; and where this is the case, domestic decency and the nicer proprieties of personal conduct are out of the question.[2]

Many old houses, such as these on Lower Redcross Street, survived in the period

In 1848, Dare drew attention to the problems associated with lodging-house residents, noting how many were youngsters who had left home early on account of overcrowding:

One great reason why the low taverns are so much frequented is that numbers of the operatives are single lodgers, having left the parental roof at an early - too early - age, or crowding in here from the surrounding villages. There is no room for such at the fireside; they are often requested, unceremoniously, to walk out awhile to give place to the regular household. If it happens to be wet, they must stand under some gateway, or, as is more frequently done, resort to the public-house. A young man, a member of our adult class, who is fond of books, informed me that he had often been forbidden to read when a lodger, as there was neither room nor candle for any such thing. Early desertion from home, too, in many instances, arises from the dwelling becoming too small for the increasing family. Think of ten or twelve huddled together in one sleeping room! Some of them are glad to fly from its loathsomeness and indecency. It is a common thing for a part of even tidy working people's children to sleep at different neighbours' houses, through the want of room at home; this custom must be dangerous to every prudent habit and feeling. Ready-furnished rooms or houses are an abominable nuisance; they offer an open receptacle for the dissolute and refractory. A young girl, the eldest of a large family, several of whom improved much in our evening school, resorted with her

Working-class slum housing: Bateman's Yard, off Sandacre Street, built c.1840 - photographed before demolition in the 1930s

paramour, and several other unmarried couples, to one of these dens of infamy.

Almost all moral manifestations arise from "circumstance," which Byron, I think, calls "an unspiritual God." How can decency or self-respect be the fruit, where ten or twelve human beings vegetate in a spot 11 feet by 9'. How difficult to cherish the parental and filial affections where there is neither food, nor clothing, nor education, or for health and cheerfulness and gratitude to flourish? Their diseases, again: the tettered head, the blotched skin, the burning fever, and icy consumption are the direct result of physical neglect. Think of dwellings standing where the doors and windows are obliged to be shut to keep out the reekings of cess-pools and hog-sties, instead of being opened to the "breezy call of incense-breathing morn!" Think of families getting up in the long dead winter nights because they could not sleep for the cold. Think of nine removals in a year! How destructive of all domestic comfort, of all prospective plans![3]

In 1852, Dare related sickness to the poor living conditions endured by many, and drew attention to working-class appeals to 'quackery', especially that practised by the 'Wise Woman of Wing':

During the intense heat of the summer, the task of visiting the sick was physically repulsive in the extreme. I shall never forget one poor old widow upon whom I called at this season. She seemed to be literally frying in her bed, which was reeking with her perspiration. This was principally caused by the ill-construction of the dwelling, which made it impossible to produce a fit temperature. The slated roof lay close upon the ceiling - the ceiling itself was a great deal too low - and the upper sash was a fixture. Such, with the additional fact of having neither back-doors nor back-windows, is the usual construction of the dwellings for the "poorest of the poor," even in this town. Just the reverse is required. The sleeping-room and roof should be a very great deal higher, and due ventilation should be secured in the very construction of the building, so that it will operate in spite of the negligence of the occupiers. This class of dwelling should be placed under the same surveillance as the lodging-houses. If the health of human beings there requires the space of a certain number of cubic feet each, they must require the same everywhere.

The private abodes of the Irish especially demand superintendence. It is a custom with them in taking a house, for one responsible person to rent it, but ten or a dozen others also make it their nightly rendezvous after their wanderings for rags and bones, and such things - or for the sale of wood in all directions. I went myself to one of these houses at the request of a benevolent gentleman, to see to the requirements of an Irishman who had been taken ill in one of his fields. I called on a Sunday morning, and then counted nine men, two women without shoes or stockings, and several children; all inmates of a place scarcely large enough for a single family. It is probable that more than these crept in here "under night's sable cloak," for Paddy Cardimugh was brought in from the street to answer my inquiries. The Scripture-reader whose especial business is to visit the Catholic Irish, informed me that as many as twenty grown-up persons may be often found herding together in these private houses. Filth, degradation, and disease are the sure results.

The completion of the Water Works will be a great blessing to the town. I have heard during the summer innumerable complaints of the failure of this indispensable element: quantity and quality are both at fault. I can speak feelingly here, for my own supply has failed every week for a long time. A person whom I regularly visit complains that fourteen houses in his locality are without a pump, and he is obliged literally to steal his water when the possessors of private pumps are out of the way. Another intelligent friend, residing in quite a different part of the town, complains of water, "not fit to drink," for his own and a dozen other households. Add to this the present abominable state of the drainage throughout the town, and we cannot wonder, though we may not cease to grieve, at the alarming sickness and mortality that, of late, have afflicted more or less all classes of the inhabitants. From the far villas on the London-road, to the extremities of "the North" and the Belgrave-gate, fever and diarrhoea have spread their desolating blight. From these and other causes vast numbers of the poor are always in a low state of health. This is no doubt the reason why they are perpetually seeking after the nostrums of quackery. Of course, I have

Working-class housing, Green Street, built c.1840

heard of the "Wise Woman of Wing." The London Board, by its dilatoriness and needless objections to the proposed Drainage Scheme, has been the best patron she has had in this neighbourhood; for many here who visit her have no positive disease, but are oppressed with that languid disenjoyment of existence consequent upon malaria and undrained dwellings. So, a long ride into the country, with a change of scenery, food, and fresh air, with a dose of peppermint and senna, really seems to do them good for a little while. Were not the notions which the poor form of her power lamentable, they would be truly laughable. Epileptic fits and idiocy, withered limbs and carious bones, hydrocephalus and flatulency, are all submitted to her "cantrip slight;" so that "between wind and water" she drives a pretty good trade. Parties of ten or twelve are frequently going from Leicester to this "seventh daughter of the seventh daughter of the seventh daughter;" and the most ludicrous accounts are constantly told me of her curative powers. A poor woman whose consumptive son has made the journey twice, tells me the Wise Woman has cured "a born idiot who never walked or talked of six years," - that she "restored a withered arm," and was "nearly as good as our Saviour for cures."

But, to be serious, the prevalence of so many diseases from preventible causes is a sad reflection on a Christian age. There is scarcely a family, up to a certain point in the social scale, that has not thus had to mourn over the sickness or loss of some of its members. It is quite distressing at times to visit amongst them. I have officiated at the Cemetery when as many as sixteen children have been buried in one day. The districts of the poor in this town are become a very Rama, filled with the lamentation and weeping of mothers over the loss of their little ones. The Meadow, which is the usual play-ground and breathing-space for the lower side of the town, is wholly unfit for such purposes - for, being clipped in by the river and the canal, it is filled with pestilential effluvia the greater part of the year. Only for two or three months in the Spring is the river endurable.[4]

Dare was still lamenting the poor living conditions suffered by many of Leicester's working classes in the 1860s:

In illustration: here is a building with no back opening, with two small rooms, one down, one upstairs. In this confined hole, a father and mother and six children herd together. The two oldest are grown-up - one a man, the other a woman. The youngest child is scarcely out of arms. They have occasionally harboured a man as a lodger. In another house with small back rooms in addition, thirteen persons, males and females, are heaped together. One of the latter brings home her paramours from the pavement. In another place, a sort of "upper room," a wife and husband and six children ferment together. Cooking, washing, sleeping, in short, all the household work has to be carried on in the same compartment. The poor stunted little ones can have no outlet for play or fresh air, for this wretched cage is cooped up behind respectable buildings and shut off from the street by a narrow passage, through which rags and squalor may not pass. Cupidity here seems totally blind, for is it to be wondered at if disease should issue from such a place and desolate the neighbourhood? Can health, decency, or religion be nurtured in such hot-beds? If, as is properly the case, in common lodging houses, a certain number of cubic feet of space must be allowed to each individual, why not enforce the same rule wherever it is violated?[5]

Working-class slum housing: Rathbone Place, off East Street, built c.1840

Dare also drew regular attention to the way poor working conditions had an adverse effect on health and behaviour. He considered the issue in some detail in 1862:

I called one day to see a member of our adult class. She had the last few days brought home her work. There was a visible change in her appearance. Her mother observed, "Lizzie could stand it no longer to work in such a place. She and some of the other girls are often taken out fainting." Her brother died of decline. She would have fallen a victim herself had not timely care been taken and means obtained to send her to the seaside. An intelligent fancy-hand informs me that he "worked in a shop in this town where forty men were employed from fourteen to sixteen hours a day, without any ventilation except opening the windows, which was next to impracticable, and always dangerous. In the depth of winter forty gas-lights would be burning for six hours without any outlet for the smoke, until the place was like the "black hole at Calcutta." "I have had to go," he continues, "downstairs literally by the hour for breath, and in the morning have expectorated matter tinged with soot." Smaller shops are yet worse, and frequently they are clouded with tobacco smoke, and many instead of rushing out for fresh air, seek the public-house from sheer exhaustion, so that the love of strong drink is often created by a low physical condition. The finishing department too of the new kind of shoemaking must be very prejudicial. As there is no stitching, the workmen can sit nearly close together. This they do at both sides and ends of a low bench that reaches the whole length of a small narrow room. As heated irons are scarcely ever out of their hands, gas is always burning on a level with their knees, sitting on low seats. The walls and ceilings are all black with gas smoke. An intelligent friend tells me that "seven finishers work in a room about 10 feet by 8 feet; mouth of the chimney boarded up; no ventilation except at the door when opened for ingress or egress; four gas-lights by night and two in the day to heat the burnishers." "In another room," he says, "about 8 feet square, with a bed in it, and no fire-place; two gas-lights always burning, four finishers work; the bench occupying nearly the whole of the spare room; the workmen are compelled to sit on the bedside to work." This is the way disease is generated. All workshops should be like the factories, under inspection.[6]

All manner of disease hit Leicester in the period. Noting in 1869 that the town was scarcely free from measles, Dare wondered whether the 'inordinate consumption of swine's flesh' had anything to do with it. 'Hundreds' amongst the town's working class evidently ate no other meat than pork, bacon and pig's offal.[7] In 1874, Dare again raised the question of meat-eating, this time to consider why the working classes did not eat more of the Australian meats that were readily available:

As meat of every kind is so dear, I endeavoured to ascertain in my visits the reason why the Australian meats are not more used. Gathering at my request the opinions of his fellow working men on this subject, a very intelligent operative writes me: "There are several reasons why Australian meat does not become an article of general consumption amongst the working classes. Perhaps, first, amongst these is the question of economy. You will best understand it, if I place the Australian meat beside the usage and means of the working people. The cheapest rate at which the cooked meat can be bought is in 6lb. tins, at about 6d. per lb. You may buy a 2lb. tin for 1s. 6d., or an odd pound where they open large tins for sale for 8d. or 9d. Now let us see how this arrangement and price suits the people for whom it is intended. It is only once a week that ordinary working people buy large pieces of meat, varying from 1lb. to 6lbs., according to circumstances, and the number which must be provided for. Where the number is large and the means small, the house-wife can go to market or shop, and buy that part which best suits both in taste and pocket; and it will have this advantage over the Australian meat; it can be boiled, roasted, or fried, as most suitable. Australian meat is prime, at least, in price. But it is the week-days that tell most against its use. After

Monday the pieces become very small. Indeed, to purchase all meat comes not to the share of many; they are satisfied to get it largely mixed with offal. On week-day mornings the matron takes her 4d. or 6d. to the butcher's where she can choose a bit of coarse or a bit of breast of mutton, if the plate has not been left over night for half a sheep's head or liver. You may take a practical lesson in this on any week-day morning, if you will notice some favourite butcher's shop in a crowded neighbourhood. It may be asked, 'Why not purchase the Australian cooked meat, especially on a Saturday?' You might ask a hundred and you would get the same reply from ninety-nine: 'It goes no way,' which means it does not satisfy; a person can eat a large quantity and not feel full. This may be through its being easy of digestion, and, if so, it ought to be put as a mark in its favour. But while this is an objection amongst the poor, they think it should be its highest recommendation to the rich, as they could have it served up with all sorts of condiments, and eat their fill without any disagreeable effects. The rich certainly are the people who ought to take heartily to its use, for nothing is especially suited to the poor that is not cheap and will not 'go a long way.' Perhaps no new thing has been introduced without meeting with a certain amount of prejudice, and many women believe there is no goodness in the meat, and I have heard men of sound judgment say it is very well for tea, but not for dinner. There are some to be met with who do not like the taste of the meat, while many who do like it say they should not do so constantly. My own opinion is that Australian cooked meat will never supersede butcher's meat; and the price at which it is sold at present wholly removes it from amongst the things of every day consumption by working people. In its present form it offers no advantage whatever to them. It must be decidedly cheaper before prejudice and custom can be broken through. This is the channel in which those who are interested should direct their efforts. We have tried the mutton occasionally ourselves, and believe it contains all the goodness that meat can contain. It would be much better if meat could be brought fresh into the English market; it has been tried lately, and only requires a little further effort to become a complete success. I forgot to say earlier that in summer the Australian meat will not keep fresh after the tins are opened, and at no time is it so good as when just turned out of the tin." The necessity of buying whole tins seems to be the chief objection to the use of this meat.[8]

There were regular outbreaks of smallpox in Leicester in the period. In 1864, Dare described in detail how one such epidemic spread rapidly in the poorest districts in the town:

Common ashpit and open-pail closet, Taylor Street, 1870s - shared by about 15 families

I have ascertained that there are at least fifteen hundred dwellings in this town that have neither back doors nor windows. So that allowing five inmates to each, which will be found under the mark, as the lower the grade of the population the thicker is the crowding together, there are no less than between seven and eight thousand sweltering in these wretched unhealthy abodes. The habits too of the inmates of back yards and confined courts, are altogether different from those who live in sunlight and fresh air. Seldom seen by respectable people, they are heedless both of personal appearance and domestic cleanliness. From the common use of the same filthy "midden" and vulgar familiarities amongst themselves, gossiping in common at each other's houses, they lose all decency of manners and sink into both moral and physical corruption. Hence it will be seen that moral causes have much to do with the sanitary condition of towns. In addition to scarlatina, typhus fever, and measles, it is too well known that small-pox spread its fearful ravages widely amongst us. In the course of my visits, I had necessarily to call on many afflicted with this loathsome disease. All the cases I met with were in very close dwellings, some of them without back openings, and the others apparently over-crowded, as in one house I found four grown-up persons who suffered from it, the father dying; in another confined dwelling four had it, three of them adults; in another house with no back ventilation, four children died. I never before found so many ill of this terrible malady. The impression amongst many was that this disease was brought to the town in the leather. Most likely this idea arose from the fact that several shoemakers were amongst its first victims. And this fact shows that personal habits have much to do with the origination of the disease, for with grief it must be stated this class are amongst the most degraded of the working population. Many of the finishing shops are wholly destructive of health. But however the disease was introduced into the town, there can be no doubt that it was disseminated pretty freely when once it had gained a footing. It was lamentable to observe the want of forethought and care exhibited by

A working-class court off Burley's Lane from the period, photographed before demolition in the 1930s

those who are attacked. A father dies of this virulence in full habit, and is kept in a small close room, the only sleeping apartment, for three days, before interment; the inevitable consequence is that others of the family take the poison into their veins. I knew such a case. Three of his children, all adults, who had been vaccinated fell ill, and one of them nearly lost her life. I remember when I was a boy we lived on the skirts of a common, where there was a house bearing the ominous, and to children, dreadful name of "The pest house." To this building all cases of fever and small-pox were sent as soon as discovered. No doubt this plan would greatly check these preventible and repulsive maladies. Now, if we cannot re-build pest-houses, at least all the more virulent cases, especially where the corpses have to remain in small pent up rooms, might be immediately removed to the mortuary at the cemetery. Another way in which this disease is spread is in this manner. A person, an adult, whose occupation is to crochet round the borders of large surfaces of fancy hosiery, many of which pieces from the delicacy of their texture require nice and intricate manipulation, falls ill of the small-pox. She has them very badly. The family is needy. The small earnings are required to carry on from hand to mouth. As soon therefore as the disease is turned, and before the pustules have dried off, the patient gets to work at her fancy fabrics. A few scales are scratched off, a few stitches set, and so on, till the picture becomes too sickening for representation. Before well recovered, a sister takes them, and goes through the same sick and sickening process. And thus for two months the whole of the work from a large shop passes through this sink of pestilence. Without any cleansing process these articles are sent into the market. Some of them so infected are purchased by delicate ladies, who become ill, and perhaps disfigured for life, wondering however they caught the infection. In another visit I found three half-grown children in one bed. The oldest was a girl of sixteen, another of fourteen, and a boy of twelve. All three had this disgusting disease, the boy very badly. In opposition to my wish the father stirred them up, lifting his son forward by putting his arms closely round his body, and baring his limbs, so that his hand must necessarily be soiled. But without washing them he resumed his work of tailoring, making perhaps some garment that would be put on as soon as done, and the disease would thus be introduced, into some respectable family. Children too are suffered to play with others, or to go to school too soon after their illness, especially as little care is taken to cleanse either the body or its covering. I was talking one day with a poor woman about her child who had died of this fearful malady. She said, he would go into the next door neighbour's whose little boy "had them very bad," and drink out of the mug that held his "toast and water"; the child had not been vaccinated, and consequently caught the small-pox and died. "But," she added, "I did not think it any use to keep my child away, for God could find him out wherever he was, as well as He did the other." Thus ignorance, and filth, and fatalism, sow the seeds of disease broad-cast through the land. In this loathsome disease too when death is apprehended, a minister of religion is sent for, often by some officious person unknown to the patient. What an erroneous conception of religious ministration does this betray! How can a person attend to devotion when the poisonous virulence is seething through his veins, his brain ready to burst, and only an hour or so of life remaining?[9]

The issue of compulsory vaccination against smallpox was a highly sensitive one to Leicester's working-class population. Dare considered the problem in 1869:

I find in my visits, that there is amongst the poor a very strong objection to Compulsory

Vaccination. With the view of ascertaining the reason of their dislike and strong opposition to this measure, we have invited the working men to a discussion in our class. There seems to be a growing impression amongst them that vaccination from one child to another causes eruptive affections, either implanting or developing scrofulous and other cutaneous diseases of a disgusting nature. Several have submitted to be fined and imprisoned rather than have their offspring vaccinated. The same opposition prevails in all our large towns. The leaders of the opposition are the herbalists or "Electric Practitioners." Several invited took part in the discussion. They managed their case very creditably. I have looked over some of their writers against the present practice; but others amongst the educated faculty strongly advocate Jenner's plan; - so who shall decide when doctors disagree? I tell mothers, in my visits, that at any rate the Queen submits her children to vaccination. But after all, my conviction is, that unless the public vaccinator exercises great care, there is much danger of communicating hereditary taints, for these inquiries showed that they were widely spread amongst certain classes. But while this agitation is going on in England, they are demanding compulsory vaccination in California, New Zealand, and Queensland, and I believe in India, where the small-pox is spreading its loathsome ravages. A remarkable contribution to the controversy now in progress, as to the merits of vaccination, is furnished by an official body in Ireland. The Poor Law Commissioners there have, it seems, informed the Belfast Board of Guardians, that small-pox has altogether ceased in the sister country. This result the Commissioners attributed to the careful carrying out of the Compulsory Vaccination Act, enforced in Ireland since 1863. The figures given are very striking. Before that year, the deaths from small-pox averaged 1000 annually; in 1864 the number was reduced to 854; in 1865, it was 347; in 1866, 189; in 1867, 20; and in 1868 only 19 deaths occurred. In the first quarter of 1869 there were none. In the interest of science and health, it is to be hoped that we shall hear what measures were adopted to obtain pure lymph, and whether any other causes had a share in promoting the happy result.[10]

In 1866, drawing attention to the increase of measles, fever and consumption in the town, Dare noted the indifference of landlords to improve working-class living conditions:

The autumn was not so sickly as many are, but the winter, though not so cold as often experienced, was plashy and ungenial, causing considerable mortality amongst the very old and very young. Measles and fever lurked about, and consumption, the scourge of our country, seems to be continually on the increase. I have constantly several cases on hand. Two or three persons, so afflicted, have lately hastened their own death by submitting to modes of treatment advised by a London practitioner. His method is by inhalation of vapours, repeated applications of a number of leeches to the throat, chest, &c., thereby exhausting, instead of strengthening the constitution. I have met with some cases of fever that were evidently generated by the domestic habits of its victims. In a house in a closed back yard, with one up and one down door room, a father and mother, six children, some of them 16 or 17 years of age, and a grown-up young man herd together. Three of the children have had fever, and the youth has been in the Infirmary, in consumption. Fever, more or less severe, has frequently appeared in this household. When the small-pox was raging in the town the family living next door, in the same kind of den, suffered from this hideous malady. I asked the father why he did not go to a larger house? He said he had tried to obtain one, but landlords will not let property where there are large families. To make matters worse, there were actually two or three hens sitting under the stairs - so this dirty, confined place serves for coal-hole, pantry, and fowl-pen. There was also a poor thrush in a seldom-cleaned cage, and, of course, a dog and cat or two about. In another case of fever, I observed that there was always a quantity of decaying vegetable matter about the house, arising from the sale of garden productions. In another case the father of a family was taken to the fever house, and died. The wife thought, very properly, that the house should be well cleaned, as it had not been whitewashed for seven years. But the house-agent peremptorily refused to have it done, and threatened her with immediate expulsion if she made any to do about it. Nothing is done, she leaves; another family comes in and inherits the filth and disease of the pre-occupiers, through the ignorance and inhumanity of the collector. Landlords, who often reside at a distance, are unacquainted with such circumstances, and others, who are needy and penurious, wink at them. I visited two other cases, both of very aged men, one was upwards of eighty, and the other more than ninety. They were both at lodging houses; the parish allowed one 2s. 6d. per week, but refused to assist the other. Both, without doubt, would have been better in the Union house, for it was evident that the lodging-house keepers made a hand of their sickness, getting drink with what was left in charity. But I allude chiefly to these two lodging houses, situated in distant parts of the town, to express my utter disgust at the filthy condition of the rooms where these two poor old men were counting out their last pulses of life.[11]

The issue of Leicester's high mortality rate, especially among the very young, increasingly came to dominate Dare's reporting on health matters by the 1870s. In 1873, he put forward a range of explanatory factors for the problem:

Much has been said, and something is now being done, in reference to the frightfully high mortality amongst the very infants in our town. The causes apparently have not been discovered, or, if so, though most of them preventible, they have not been removed - a state of things not very creditable to any whom it may concern. With the view of testing my own experience and judgement in this matter, I inquired of a medical gentleman, who kindly submitted the following as his convictions, confirmed by nearly twenty years' practice amongst "the innocents":

"One of the chief causes is to be found in the fact that marriages are contracted at much too early an age, without any household preparation whatever, even 'prentice-boys' rush into this responsible condition. The great prosperity of the more easily learned trades of the town, at which young people, mere boys and girls, have been able to get high wages, has made them impatient of all restraint, and, as a consequence, marriage has been decided upon. The physical and mental constitutions of neither parties being properly developed before children are born to them, what can be expected from such unions but such children as we so frequently meet with, poor, weakly, sickly, fragile things, with not more than half the vitality they ought to possess, to enable them to combat the various ailments to which infancy and childhood are exposed. As a consequence, they bear badly such diseases as measles, small-pox, whooping-cough, scarlatina, or diarrhoea, whilst healthy, robust children shake them off, and without any of the after-consequences which befall the former. Another cause is the wretched nursing these fragile little creatures suffer, being left sometimes to poor old women, sometimes to mere children whilst the mothers are gone out to work; they are then drugged with carminatives, Godfrey's, or soothing powders, and so administered as to produce stupefaction just the time of the mother's absence; and in addition, what is almost as destructive, the feeding-bottle, never half cleansed, and full of some starchy preparation, as corn-flour or arrowroot, boiled with water instead of pure new milk, is kept constantly in the child's mouth. The mother suckles the babe before leaving it in the morning, and when she returns to her meals; the starchy preparation, or bread boiled with water, is given to the infant under the ignorant impression - obtained from the grandmother or the nurse - that 'two milks' do not agree; the consequences of this drugging and stuffing, and that lack of comfort which can only be imparted by the mother, are debility, atrophy, convulsions, diarrhoea, &c., ending most frequently in death, or if it survive all this management, the child grows up a puny, sickly thing, suffering from indigestion, mal-assimilation, &c."

"Another cause which has been partly hinted at, is the ignorant notion that the little ones are to be kept in health by perpetual recurrence to all manner of nostrums, many of which are of a mineral nature, and based upon preparations of mercury, and antimony, calomel, grey powder, or James's fever powder, which is a compound preparation of antimony. These are favourite but too often fatal remedies. Another cause, if not vaccination, is its too early use amongst the naturally debilitated and weakly little ones. A deficient sanitary condition of the homes of certain classes has always been a fruitful source of disease and premature death. Numbers are overcrowded and there are still hundreds of houses where the top sash of the window will not open, and in the bedrooms no means of ventilation either by window or fireplace; this ought not to be allowed; the rent paid ought to ensure houses fit for human beings to inhabit, instead of not being fit for animal life at all."[12]

In 1875, drawing attention to the increased number of working mothers in Leicester, Dare argued how inimical to infant care and health this situation was:

In view of the excessive mortality of the "little ones" that has so long distressed the town, and which must show that its causes are not yet well understood, a medical gentleman recently inquired of me "whether married female labour had not lately much increased?" I have made many inquiries amongst different branches of labour, and the general impression seems to be that it has much increased of late years. An intelligent co-worker well acquainted with the subject states, "My opinion is that the number of married women who go out to work is greatly upon the increase, and for the following reasons. First, the introduction of machinery, making labour comparatively light, is the cause of a larger demand for female labour, as, for instance, thirty years ago there was only one female employed in our establishment. Now there are no less than 124, and most of them are doing work with new and improved machinery, which was done by men only at one time. Women's wages are much higher, and I think have increased more after the rate than men's. Consequently when they get married they are loth to leave work till they are obliged through confinement or temporary cause, and then they are always encouraged to return as soon as the cause of absence is surmounted. Then, secondly, there are other trades now besides fancy hosiery which ebb and flow, and have what are called "busy seasons," and married women are often preferred, because they will come at any sacrifice and work hard through a busy season, and then leave work in flat times without grumbling or going to seek another job, knowing they shall be sent for as soon as there is work for them;

besides which it saves the trouble of teaching new hands. Out of the 124 females working at our place, there are 28 married persons, or nearly 25 per cent." From these facts it may be seen why married female labour is preferred.

The following account is from another standpoint, and plainly shows how inimical to infant life the social habits referred to must necessarily be. My female informant states, "I think the labour of married women is on the increase. I have looked round our place and I can only find two that have given up their work at the time of their marriage out of twenty or more. The fact is they get married too young. One fellow-worker was only seventeen, and her husband eighteen; he was serving his time somewhere as an apprentice, and would not be out of his time till he was twenty-one. His wages were eight shillings, and hers seven shillings and sixpence a week. They had no home nor any furniture, so were obliged to crowd in with his mother, which must be destructive of both health and decency. Another girl I asked at the time she was going to be married, if she had a home to go to? 'Oh! no, but we shall soon get one, he can get good money when he likes;' but I said, how often does he like? 'Why,' she says, 'I know he never thinks of working on Mondays, and sometimes not on Tuesdays, but if he will only keep to his work and me to mine we shall be "all right," adding 'we are going to live with my mother.' She was only nineteen. I thought, poor thing! you are not looking much to the future; but it was no use talking to her, she would not see that such a course was wrong. I lay a deal of the blame on the girls themselves, for I think they might see much imprudence if they would. The other day when I was going to my work, there were a couple walking just behind me. They were not married but were expecting to be. He asked her for some money; she told him she had none. 'Then,' he replied, 'if you don't give me sixpence I shan't go to work to-day,' so at last she gave him the money. Now what can that girl expect if she marries that low fellow but a life of misery, want, sickness, and the premature death of her children? I heard another low fellow say he should not go to work that day, and if he did not go all the week he should get something to eat, for his wife worked at the factory." But we need not particularise further. I am assured that, taking one factory with another, about half the female workers are married.

Now it appears from these statements that may be relied on, that married female labour is often sadly misapplied. In many cases the idle drunken husband lives on the wife's earnings, the household affairs are neglected, and the poor babes have little chance of surviving.[13]

Finally, after much deliberation on the issue of child mortality, Dare concluded in 1876 that more weight had to be given to the 'moral side' of the question:

I must say one word upon the distressing amount of infantile mortality that has so long afflicted our town. Very earnest and laudable efforts have been made to discover its causes, and the medical gentlemen engaged in the investigation must have pointed out many of them. But without presuming to controvert their conclusions, I am led by long experience to say that I do not think they have discovered the chief causes, or, at least, have not placed them before us. The moral side of the question is totally ignored. The causes of infant mortality are not to be found alone in the new houses built upon newly-made soil, for an equal sanitary authority asserts that upwards of twenty years ago it bore similar proportions to the population as it does at present, and that was before a single new house of the kind had been erected. One great cause, if not the chief cause, will be found in the vice and immorality, the drink, bad food, and irregular habits of numbers of the human family; these undermine the constitution, and physically incapacitate their victims. Then, again, hundreds of poor girls have grown up without due motherly care and guidance. From childhood their clothing, food, and hours of rest have not been duly cared for. When become independent, they waste their wages in expensive finery; and as soon as work is over, visit many questionable resorts for amusement, and, I am sorry to add, drink. From this neglect of moral and motherly training, they are destitute of the domesticities that should form them to become strong and capable mothers. The infants of such possess no sufficient vitality to surmount the maladies to which they are subjected. The uncleansed bottle, and poisonous drugs, under one name or another are, though illegal, purchasable and largely administered by this class. A friend, who has lately come into a druggist's shop, informs me that he was astonished at the constant inquiry for laudanum, and he noted many of the cases. One young woman stated that she was in the constant habit of using it. As much as ninepennyworth a week, and sometimes more. It was painful to see her low moral condition. Another, quite an elderly woman, was greatly surprised that I would not sell it; she had used it for a number of years; she seemed conscious that she was under its influence at the time, and in fact, it has gained quite the mastery over her. She ended her altercations by saying, "While I can get it, I will have it." He referred also to overcrowding and defective air. It is in this direction that we must look for the causes of untimely mortality. I concur in much of Dr. Nuttall's report, as well as in that of Messrs. Buck and Franklin, and from equally long experience fully endorse the conclusions of Mr. Hawksley, uttered at the late Social Science Congress. "For thirty years I have devoted

Leicester Infirmary, 1850s

myself to the investigation of this important question, and have finally arrived at the conclusion - a conclusion based on statistical research and personal observation - that the natural term of life of our urban population is unnaturally shortened by preventible causes to the extent of one-fifth, and that these preventible causes are to be sought not in the water pipes and sewers, but chiefly in the houses and habits of the industrial classes."[14]

Throughout his *Reports*, Dare referred to the improvements made to public health and living conditions in Leicester. One voluntary measure which drew his particular commendation was the setting up of a new Dispensary in 1866. Following a visit he made to the establishment in 1868, he reported on its aims and operations, at the same time drawing attention to problems with the functioning of the Infirmary:

Having been kindly invited to look over the Dispensary I went a few weeks ago. The manager, Mr. Dalrymple, conducted me very courteously through the establishment. As far as I can judge I think it admirably adapted for its purpose. There is a nice office for issuing tickets and receiving subscriptions. The books are kept in an excellent manner, and will show at a glance for a hundred years to come the number of patients admitted. The laboratory and work rooms, not forgetting the dentist's apartment, are all very convenient, and communicate with the waiting room, which is a nice airy comfortable place. Here all applicants assemble; those seeking admission turn to a private opening to the office, those wanting medicines to an opening where they are prepared, and those receiving medicine to another near the outlet. This is a very nice arrangement, completely obviating the complaints I used to hear about the old building, where all had to crowd to one point that "was like the trap door of the relieving officer." When patients are too ill to attend, the medical officers wait upon them at their own homes, which is an inestimable blessing to the sick. I have heard them speak of it in the most affectionate and grateful manner. Upwards of twenty thousand prescriptions have been dispensed, and advice given in nearly ten thousand cases. There are more than five thousand on the books, and I understood from the manager that fifteen or twenty thousand could be effectually attended to. Surely working men will secure these important advantages for themselves, and those who are dependent on them. As home visiting is the great desideratum of the Infirmary, and as its income is deficient, would it not be well that it should cease to issue out-patient tickets? Many of them are now literally thrown away, through the holders of them being too weak to go, or continue going such long journeys to that excellent establishment. It should either have a central depot or give up its out-patients to the Dispensary, which could find room for them all. The latter is fast realising the end of a self-supporting institution, and deserves every encouragement.[15]

The establishment of another voluntary body, the Trained Nurses Institution, in 1867, also attracted Dare's praise:

It is very gratifying that the proposed institution for trained nurses is now in action. Mrs. Walker

The staff of Leicestershire Lunatic Asylum (now the University) c.1880

has kindly furnished the following interesting outlines of its plans. "About a year ago, a society was formed and funds collected for the purpose of sending to London intelligent young women of good character to be thoroughly trained in the hospitals there and afterwards brought to Leicester, some to nurse the poor gratuitously, and others to go out as salaried, private nurses. The undertaking has so far been attended with the happiest results. Four young women have had a year's training in London. In one out of the five districts into which the town has been divided, the nurse has been at work two months to the perfect satisfaction of the committee. Three other districts are about to have the same advantages immediately, so that, before the close of this year, four fifths of the town will have the services of trained nurses. The duties of these nurses are to go from house to house, to carry out the doctors' orders, and to see that sanitary regulations are properly attended to, and by their skill and experience to alleviate suffering; also to supply medical comforts, such as wine, beef tea, &c., which may be necessary to the recovery of the sick, which they may not be able to procure. I am happy to say, this work of christian charity has been taken up and supported without respect of creed or opinion. To ministers of religion of all denominations, to medical men and others, will be given power to recommend suitable patients for the nurses' care, such persons as need not go to the Infirmary, or workhouse, and who yet require help and nursing. It must not be overlooked that the nurse will be an educator, as well as a dispenser of charity, and that the poor will learn from her the best way of nursing each other. It is to be hoped that this enterprise to help our suffering neighbours will meet with wide and generous support." This institution, if judiciously carried on, will confer incalculable blessings upon the sick and needy. The better teaching of the nurses will do away in some degree with quackery and superstition, as to remedial measures, and correct absurd notions about charms. There may be a little truth underlying some of these, such for instance, as taking a child in the whooping cough into the fields, till a bramble or briar be found with both ends, growing in the ground, then taking the patient nine mornings and putting the child while repeating certain words, nine times over and under it; for as fresh air is necessary to recovery, the working of the charm secures it. You must go a long way perhaps before you can find a bramble, so formed, and the nine mornings' walk will give "their breezy calls and incense-breathing" scenery. But some methods are so disgusting that one can scarcely believe that a mother should take a delicate child in the whooping cough and hold it over a cesspool till vomiting is produced by stirring up its nauseous gases.[16]

Dare also recommended that the Institution have a 'baby branch' on the lines of one operating in Westminster. It would improve nursing facilities for working mothers by serving as a crèche:

It should be near a sufficient number of the factories and warehouses to guarantee its usefulness. I quite believe there would be no lack of sympathy on the part of the upper classes if the thing could be made practicable. I mentioned the project to another kind-hearted woman, who has a Saviour's love for the "little ones," having brought up several babies, belonging to mothers who worked at factories, in such a way as to frequently call forth my admiration. She jumped at the idea, knowing how much suffering it would obviate, and felt assured that if properly managed the institution might be nearly, if not altogether, made self-supporting. "Bless God for little children," says Mary Howitt, and so says every Christian heart. It is chiefly by attending to the neglected portions of the rising generation that society will be improved. While making inquiries on this subject I was delighted to find that an attempt of the kind has been carried out in Westminster. Mr. James Greenwood, in the Morning Star, gives the following account of it: - "In Peter-lane, getting towards Tufton-street, there is a quiet looking house, in a row with the others. It has a shop, but the windows are now partially whitened, and nothing now is sold there. On the door is a notification that this is the infant nursery, all information concerning which may be obtained on ringing the bell. I rang the bell, and a decent-looking young woman answered, and in reply to my inquiry civilly informed me that the matron was not at home, but that I was very welcome to look over the establishment. The shop and parlour appeared to be used as a sort of office and living room, in one. The young woman took me upstairs to the first floor, where one of the oddest sights it was ever my lot to witness immediately met my view. In the front room, which is a large one, there is a space in the middle railed round, like a miniature horse circus, the rail being about eighteen inches high, a netting of string extending from it to the floor. Spread within this ring was, first a wool mattress, then an India rubber sheet, and over all a warm woollen rug. This was where the babies, the tiny things from a month old up to toddling size, disported, and there they were disporting - happy and contented, seemingly, as birds in a nest. Toddling about the room, which was plentifully furnished with comfortable little chairs, were several other little children, all with clean faces and well brushed hair, and all wearing an ample pink pinafore, with the sleeves tied up with a lot of blue ribbon. There were toys to play with, and pictures on the walls, and a swing, and a magnificent rocking chair, presented by some kind patron; and, somehow, the decent little woman in charge of them had such a capital way of managing them that they were all as merry as grigs, and in the best of humours one towards the other. Out of this room you came to one still prettier, for here, ranged along the walls were tiny iron cots, with white sheets and feather pillows; and this is where the youngsters, tired of play, were laid to rest on afternoons. There was one so resting now, with an elephant out of Noah's Ark in his chubby hand. The civil young woman took me a little higher in the house, and showed me a lead flat, securely railed in, and on one side were growing some blooming scarlet runners. This was the babies' play ground. She took me to another room, which was the bathing room, and the water closets were here, too, but without the faintest smell, a fact accounted for, probably, by the existence of a capacious cistern, as large as many in the neighbourhood that had to do duty for an alley of twenty houses. And when I had seen all that was to be seen the civil young woman told me what it all meant. Five years ago some kind ladies in the neighbourhood, pitying the shocking condition of the little children, such as I have endeavoured to describe, and knowing that the mischief arose chiefly out of the circumstance of their mothers being compelled to be out at work from morning till night, laid their heads together and opened this babies' home. They undertook the charge of the little children from a month old and upwards, from seven in the morning till eight at night, to feed, tend, nurse, and wash them for the sum of threepence per day. And ever since they stuck to the good work, with what blessed result who can tell? The average attendance at the nursery, I was informed, is twenty. They have received as many as thirty, and, without doubt, the greater part of these, had they not been snatched from it, would have been shock-headed, black-legged gutter grovellers, like the poor little wretches to be seen all round about. I have reason to believe that the good ladies who started and persevered in this noble work would do more if they had the means, for it need not be told that threepence a day per subject does not pay expenses or nearly. It is not only the food that has to be bought. These pink pinafores, for instance, were provided that the babies might appear uniformly decent; and the feather pillows for the tired little heads were not procured without money. On public grounds this tiny institution has a claim on public charity, especially at this season, for who knows how much its exertions have effected toward keeping the neighbourhood free of cholera?"

I feel convinced that if a better race is to be reared the babies must be taken in hand. It is simply a disgrace to a wealthy and Christian country, that more than half the little ones of the working class are swept away in infancy.[17]

In his *Reports*, Dare also drew brief attention to the improvements made to health and environment under the auspices of the local Board of Health. He notes, for instance: the improved sewerage system and water supplies;[18] the property inspection and whitewashing during the cholera epidemic in 1865-6;[19] the improved cleansing of streets and flushing of drains;[20] the building of wider streets; the improved prevention of nuisances; the passing of bye-laws aimed at the construction of better working-class housing;[21] the destruction of 'untaxed dogs' in 1866, which he considered both a health and moral hazard;[22] the efforts being made to discover the causes of Leicester's notoriously high rate of mortality, especially amongst infants.[23]

It is clear that throughout most of the period,

Dannett Street housing, built late 1860s, early 1870s. Dare referred to the 'scamped tenements' built in the vicinity

however, Dare remained very critical of local Board of Health policy. Indeed, most of his detailed reporting on the Board's work is highly disparaging. In 1872, for instance:

When the Medical Board ceases to tamper merely with effects and symptoms, there may be some hope that it will discover and root out the causes of disease. Scientific nomenclatures and classifications of disease are of little avail. The medical servants of Boards of Health, duly remunerated, and not allowed private practice, should go into their labours like missionaries, visiting and re-visiting the whole town by house-row, and personally inspecting all kinds of buildings, and every hole and corner of human habitation. Overcrowding, dilapidation, cleansing, water, drainage, ventilation, &c., &c., might then be properly investigated. This may possibly be thought by some beneath their dignity, but other towns have adopted the plan with great advantage; and it must be adopted here, if disease and death are to be kept within their natural limitations. There are plenty of men possessing the necessary qualifications, who would pursue this method from love to their fellow-creatures, and the satisfaction of securing to them the greatest of all earthly blessings - health.

Our confined courts are the nurseries of vice, disease and death. They are becoming more and more so from year to year. The greater number of these places, when first built, were open on some sides to the "breath of heaven." Leicester was formerly noted for gardens and intra-mural spaces; these are fast disappearing. Yards and courts are being more closely surrounded, overshadowed by factories and blank walls, till the very air and sunlight are excluded as not belonging to our common humanity. Think of thirty or forty individuals using the same recess, and this dammed up at the back with the filth and refuse of a number of dwellings without back doors or windows, and placed only a few feet from the entrances to these "Mount Pleasants," or "Spring Gardens," or "Paradise Rows," as the case may be. I know that many of these sinks have not been emptied during the whole of the summer. I could point to wholesale small-pox in one yard, to consumption in another, to baby mortality in a third, and to measles and scarlatina everywhere. While our present insanitary condition continues, our Councillors, instead of erecting ornamental and official buildings at enormous cost, should lay out the sums in the purchase and demolition of these lurking places of pestilence and immorality.

It is discouraging to observe that in several of the newly-built parts of the town, as between Flora-street and Clara-street on King Richard's-road, and other localities, there are inter-buildings springing up between the streets as originally laid out. Rows of small scamped tenements approached from the main street, through narrow arched passages, choke up what ought to be gardens and breathing spaces, and completely destroy the comfort and convenience, to say nothing of the health, of the first possessors. Each row so inter-built necessarily confines the backs of itself and at least two other rows of houses. The land as at first laid out was not intended to be thus glutted up by an inferior class of dwellings. I know some who bought and built upon it with this understanding. All this is very bad; and if our "bye-laws" sanction such crowding of habitations, so much the worse for the bye-laws, which in this respect must be amended, or the town will still be notorious for its unhealthy condition.

The following extract from the Report of the Medical Officer for Birkenhead is singularly applicable to our Borough:-

"The large increase of deaths, extending to nearly all diseases, over almost every age, and

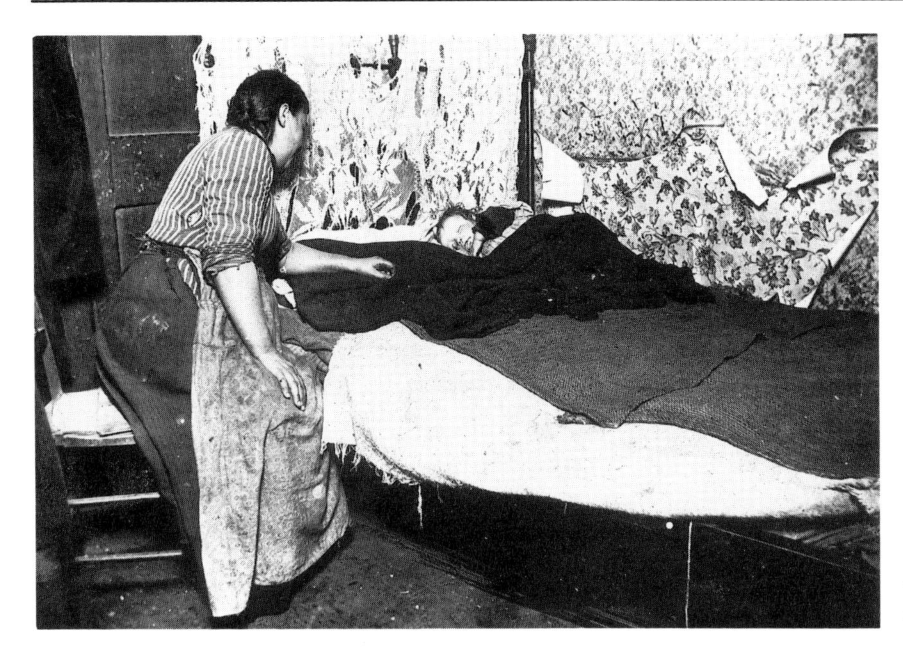

A caring hand amidst poverty

throughout each season, as well as the apparently exceptional concentration of Zymotic deaths, are quite conformable as results to what might arise from continued deficiency in the ordinary large sanitary operations of the town, and it may be conceded that, owing to various unfavourable circumstances - the night-soil removal contract, the scavenging of the streets, and the complete removal of road-scrapings and refuse, have all been much less extensively and efficiently carried on during the year and previous six months. The reduction, &c., of the inspectorial staff, has also not only materially interfered with the prompt discovery and abatement of nuisances, but has allowed to deteriorate the improved sanitary habits formerly instilled in the mass, and afterwards kept up by the constant, though friendly, pressure exercised on them by efficient inspection. A good officer is a veritable missionary of health. The important bye-law that all housekeepers should keep their portions of footpath clean, too, seems to have fallen altogether into disuse; thus retaining and hoarding the lightest organic, and generally the most putrid, dust for constant inception into houses, and into the lungs of foot passengers. An enforcement of the bye-law, or a public provision for ensuring this important sanitary requirement, is much needed, but, as all these subjects are under the consideration of the committee, they need not be further considered here."

Exactly: for as an official report, that now deserves the name (whatever we may think of its suggestions) has been presented, I will not dwell longer on this subject, only remarking that whatever is done for this class of the population must be "self-acting," for they will not voluntarily attend to any of these matters themselves; and till the proposed plans can be accomplished, the middens should be covered over to keep the rain away, and the gases sent up and off by means of wooden tubes or chimneys.

These general remarks may seem to some to be unconnected with our labours. But they are not so; for as a fellow-missionary observes, "if we make a good impression one way, there are ten other ways by which it is undone; and so long as unfit and crowded dwellings and preventable sickness remain unaltered, so long shall we have an uphill battle to carry on."[24]

In 1873 Dare argued that the Board should adopt:

the recommendation of the following "Report of the Special Committee of the Charity Organisation Society on the Dwellings of the Poor," which was presented at the weekly meeting of the Council. It is signed by Lords Napier and Ettrick; the concluding and principal recommendation is that "Extensive and effectual powers of purchase, demolition, and direct or delegated re-construction, should be vested in the chief existing municipal authorities of London - the Corporation and the Metropolitan Board of Works - in order that they may follow the example set by the municipalities of Glasgow, Edinburgh, and other provincial cities, which have been armed by local Acts with such prerogatives, and that the Corporation and Metropolitan Board should be urged to use those powers, when obtained, in a bold and comprehensive manner, but with a special regard to the interests of the poorer members of the community."

Without some such powers Medical Boards are mere farces. Scarcely anything has been done to root out the causes of disease in this town, which is shown by the perpetual recurrence of the same maladies and mortalities, with little variation, at the same periods of the year. Miss Nightingale tells us that it is preposterous to

West Bridge, 1850s. Before the construction of the flood prevention works in the 1870s, the whole area was prone to severe flooding

think that human beings must suffer in this way. Had the enormous sums wasted on the erection of unsightly buildings, and maintaining a costly medical staff beyond the boundaries of the town, which will not root out a single cause or origin of disease, as they only deal with disease after it has broken out, been expended in demolishing unhealthy dens, stopping over-crowding, removing fever-breeding filth, enforcing due water supply, effectual drainage, &c., &c., Leicester might cease, perhaps, to be so notorious for its unhealthy condition. The physical atmosphere must be purified before the moral atmosphere can be much improved. The Builder is emphatic on this subject: - "Good ventilation is not less important than good drainage. In the eye of the law houses are not considered habitable unless they are properly drained. Neither should they be considered fit for occupation unless every room is properly ventilated also. In a sanitary point of view the one is as necessary as the other. Men and women who dwell in crowded towns, and work and sleep all their lives in close rooms without ventilation, and so continually breathe air contaminated with the waste of their bodies, go down to their graves seventeen years earlier than the men and women who live in the country, and work in the green fields, and breathe the fresh air. As the poor toilers for bread in pestiferous houses and workshops in towns are shut out from the balmy breeze and the glorious sunshine; from the sight of the primrose, and the smell of the hawthorn; from the wild bird's song in the hedgerows, and the lark's merry trill in the clear blue sky; the least those who live upon their toil can do for them is to make their homes and surroundings decent and inhabitable. There always have been, and always will be, poorer classes; that is inevitable; but there is no reason why, added to their poverty, the poor should be poisoned with foul air. It is sickening to enter some of the styes called houses, in which thousands upon thousands of human beings eke out their miserable existence."[25]

By Dare's last *Report* in 1876, however, a more optimistic impression of the environment and health is evident:

The increase of the town and inhabitants is almost fabulous. The 12,000 houses and 50,000 people have grown, the former to more than 25,000, and the latter to nearly 120,000. The dwellings of the poor are of much better construction; no industrious, sober artizan need live in an inconvenient house, none are built now back to back, or without back doors or windows, or top sashes immovable, of which I am sorry to say there are many, many hundreds in the borough. Years ago, I pointed these out in my Annual Reports, and I am very glad that our Inspectors of Nuisances have just begun to discover them.

Contrasted with the former administration of the borough, its present condition is very satisfactory, and there can be no doubt that our magistrates and councillors are earnestly striving to do the best they can for the town; the liabilites incurred are all for its improvement and benefit. We have an inexhaustible supply of good water, many dangerous parts of streets have been altered, and sanitary laws are observed in the structure of all kinds of new buildings. The completion of the "Flood Scheme", as it is called, has obviated a vast amount of discomfort and misery, and other works going on in the borough must tend to increase its salubrity.[26]

Education

As part of his Census enumerator duties in 1851, Dare undertook a survey of the educational condition of the working classes in certain districts in the town. His conclusions were alarming:

Knowing it would afford an opportunity of becoming still more closely acquainted with the educational condition of certain classes, and having been applied to, I became an enumerator at the last census. I requested six other enumerators, whom I well knew, to make private observations on the same subject in their respective districts. These seven enumeration districts were all contiguous, and contained nearly 5000 inhabitants, or about one-twelfth of the whole population. There was a singular and melancholy coincidence in the results of these inquiries, which form the concurrent testimony of several intelligent working men as to the educational position of their own class. Reference to one district will be sufficient here. It comprised about six hundred individuals. Of these there were only fifty returned as at school, and thirty-two of these were under nine years of age. The eldest at school, a solitary one, was thirteen years old. There were eighty-nine from five to fifteen, not at school. Now all these ought to have been receiving instruction; as the fifty at school and the eighty-nine not at school would make one hundred and thirty-nine; which would be just about one to every four-and-a-half of the population in this section, and this number is the well known proportion that should be under daily tuition. I did not particularly notice how many adults could not write, but judging from the filling up of the schedules, a great number could not, for many of them were filled up by the landlord or shopkeeper. Out of 129 forms, I had to fill up 21, and to correct nearly all the others. The returns from the other six districts were very similar, but showing on the whole a rather darker view of the subject. And thus it will be seen that fully two-thirds of the children who should be receiving daily instruction are not at school.[1]

Dare firmly believed that education was fundamental for working-class improvement. He consequently paid particular attention to local initiatives in working-class educational provision. Though the information he provides is scanty, he did, nevertheless, throughout his *Reports*, refer to the work of religious and other voluntary bodies in setting up day and evening educational classes, noting regularly the number of new voluntary schools being established.

In his early *Reports*, he is particularly critical of the absence of free evening classes in the town. In 1854, for instance, he attacked the local 'Band of Hope' over the issue:

Were there a general system of evening instruction throughout the town, nearly all the youth might be brought under moral training. Without this we shall make little progress. For the want of this the "Band of Hope" are not realizing the wishes of their best friends. I hear many complaints of their late hours. For the want of a useful object to act as a "cordon," many of the members send in their cards; others imagine that because they observe the pledge they have no need of further moral training or elementary instruction. Again I say let us try what can be done by laying hold of the young under a system of evening instruction carried on by friendly co-operation. Attendance should be a sine qua non of membership in the Band of Hope, and every pledged drunkard who is ignorant of elementary knowledge should be carefully taught.[2]

Dare also criticised the practice of making educational provision conditional on payment or a 'certain level of intelligence':

Holy Bones County National School children, 1870s

Reverend David Vaughan, founder of the Leicester Working Men's College in 1862

Where payments are required, the exertions of the Educator fail to reach certain portions of the community - the poorest, who require the greatest attention, are almost wholly neglected.

The literary man takes up this charge of neglect, and asks if the poor have not many healthful publications written expressly for their information and guidance? True; but the poorest, they who most need them, cannot read; and, if they could, the taxes on knowledge and the terms of admission into institutions where such works may be perused, place them beyond their reach. How many operatives, who are really so, and stocking-makers, are there in the Leicester Mechanics' Institute? These establishments are above the means of the classes that most require their softening influences.[3]

By 1869, however, Dare was more optimistic, providing details of free evening classes available in the town, together with numbers on the books:

Several commendable efforts, tending to the enlightenment of the neglected classes, have been lately organized. Free evening instruction, similar to that carried on for twenty years or more in our mission, is at last being offered in several places and under the kindly co-operation of various denominations, an efficient agent has been appointed to visit parents, and secure as far as possible, the attendance of their neglected offspring. A School of Art and Design, so much required amidst manufactories, has also been inaugurated, under auspices that promise success; and many of the day schools are opened in the evening for instruction in the sciences and higher elementary branches. But oddly enough, the hand bills announcing these movements state, in some instances, that none are admitted under "fifteen;" others not under "twelve;" and others, "none need apply but of good character." So that these advantages are all above attainment by our poor neglected "street Arabs," from seven to eight thousand of whom are receiving no school education whatever, and are thus suffered to grow up in ignorance, and consequent vice and crime. But one thing is highly commendable, the impracticable system of "parish boundaries" has been broken through by some of our clerical functionaries. Such restrictions in large towns must be positive hindrances to usefulness. In that excellent institution, "The Working Men's College," as it is called, scarcely any of the attendants reside in the parish to which it belongs. What is required to lay hold of a greater proportion of the "neglected classes," is that all the day schools and rooms used as Sunday schools in the town, should be thrown open for "free evening instruction." Books, slates, &c., belonging to these schools should be laid out for the use of the attendants. Sunday school teachers and other members of the

The first home of the Leicester Working Men's College, Union Street, 1862-69

Castle Street Church voluntary school, 1869

respective congregations, whether churchmen or dissenters, should come forward and assist in teaching, or comparatively but little will be effected by the attempt. The following return, kindly communicated by the Rev. Mr. Whitton, agent for the "free evening classes," is encouraging, but as applied to the whole town it speaks for itself.

Free evening classes, number on the books:

Sanvy Gate	*Boys*	*236*
" "	*Girls*	*166*
Carley Street	*Boys*	*103*
" "	*Girls*	*111*
Paradise Row	*Boys*	*51*
		670
Average attendance Nov. 8th, 1868.		*356*

Since this date, the average attendance has nearly doubled.[4]

Despite these efforts, however, it is clear from Dare's earliest *Reports* that he was a staunch critic of voluntaryist educational provisions. He regularly lamented the way enormous sums were spent on measures of penal servitude, contending that the money would be better spent on working-class education, which would serve as a preventive measure against vice and crime. He accordingly, persistently, called for a system of state-funded and state-supervised, unsectarian, compulsory education, accompanied by greater controls on juvenile labour. The argument is put most forcibly in his detailed assessment of the educational condition of Leicester's working-class children in 1867:

Another still more important meeting was held in April, under the presidency of the Mayor, to consider the educational condition of the town. The circular calling the meeting was signed by several influential members of the orthodox body and other gentlemen, and by nine dissenting ministers. This is encouraging and, no doubt, will eventuate in some effectual system, as it is "to be conducted on thoroughly unsectarian principles, and to be placed under Government inspection." The necessity of some more comprehensive plan of instruction will be seen from the following statements laid before the meeting: "The population of Leicester is estimated at the present time to be 85,000; which, it is assumed would give 14,000 children between the ages of six and fourteen." From a personal enquiry, made expressly with a view of ascertaining the existing educational agencies in Leicester, it seems there are about 7,600 boys and girls, including infants, on the books of the Public Schools and in Private Academies in this town; the number of infants is estimated at 700; consequently there are more than 7,000 children totally unprovided with elementary teaching in Leicester.

These are alarming facts, they speak for themselves, they show a fearful amount of neglect and ignorance, and consequent crime, drunkenness, and pauperism. And that they are not exaggerated is proved in a remarkable manner, in a lecture delivered in the Town Hall, by W. Biggs, Esq., when Mayor, about eighteen years ago. In my report for 1849 it is stated: "From my enquiries which were kindly and promptly answered, I lament to say that not half the number of children are at school that ought to be there. In a population of 56,000, there are not 6,000 children at the Daily Schools, including every kind of establishment for tuition. The Dissenters have not more than 800, and the Church not quite 2,000, at their charity and other daily schools. There is nearly the same number at all the private places of instruction, and about 700 little ones at infant, and dame schools." A comparison of these figures will show that we have made but little progress in education during the last twenty years. When the population was 56,000, there were about 6,000 children at school from 5 to 15; and now it is 85,000, there are about 7,000 at school, from 6 to 14 years of age. But these are not the worst features of the case, for the children attending our present day schools are not there on average eighteen months. The following reliable information, kindly given by Mr. Hepworth, the experienced master of our excellent day-schools, obtained with the view of laying it before the meeting held at the Town Hall, had time allowed, will still further illustrate our present educational condition. His replies to my enquiries were as follows: "What average attendance have you in both schools?" Girls 280, boys 390, total 670. "How long is the average attendance at school?" Girls and boys eighteen months. "What is the average age when leaving?" Scarcely nine years of age, boys and girls. "What is the average number passing through the schools in a year?" 600 girls, 843 boys. "What percentage stay till 14 years old?" Girls 1, boys 3 per cent. "How many days' attendance secures the capitation fee?" 100 days. "What per centage obtain it?" 80 percent. This latter number, compared with the numbers passing yearly through the schools, show that about one fourth of the children attend only about a quarter of a year. "How many children will each school accommodate?" Each school will accommodate about 500 children, making a total of 1,000; the present attendance is 670, so there is room for many more. Now, waving the desirability of having very large numbers of children together, it will be seen that there is room in these well-built schools for many more than attend. All the other day schools of the same kind, have more or less unoccupied space. The promoters of the new schools will be mistaken if they suppose the mere multiplication of schools will meet the case. Schools may be indefinitely multiplied, but this will not remove the causes of non attendance. A few may be ferreted out, but the majority of the attendants will be those who happen to reside in the localities of the new schools, and now attend school, and the few grumblers who are fond of change. Nothing short of a compulsory system will force our 7,000 town Arabs into any school. All juvenile labour must be organized in some way, at least in all our large towns. Why should the dishonest employer, the extortionate middle man, the drunken journeyman, the reckless finisher, the maker of bricks, the needy householder, and numerous others, not to mention heartless parents, be privileged to work children under the age of admission to the regularly inspected factory? It is placing the humane employer at a disadvantage, for the poor little things who are not under inspection, are set to work at 7 or 8 years of age, at merely nominal wages, and kept at their drudgery from 6 in the morning till 9 or 10 at night. I have talked to brick yard boys, sweaters, winders, and others, who have told me they "were going of eight." Hence it may be inferred that there are about 6,000 juveniles at employments not under Government inspection. It is sad to think that these portions of the rising generation do not know what childhood means. They have no joyous sunny period of youth. They are forced into precocious manhood. The passions soon grow predominant. Low habits and ill connections are formed. Ale and tobacco become the summum bonum of life, and too often violence and crime mark the downward course. While this mass of ignorance and corruption is left to fester in our midst, the various moral and religious agencies amongst us cannot effect half their legitimate influence. Missing links and Bible women, Scripture readers, temperance agents and missionaries, find more than they can do in dealing merely with the symptoms of the social and moral anomalies that afflict society. In pleading for compulsory education and organization of juvenile labour, no untried principles are advocated. In the "half time system," and in all our Union workhouses, gaols, and Reformatories, they have long been in successful operation. In the name of God let them be extended to all our poor neglected children! In reference to this subject, our good Bishop in his recent charge, spoke encouragingly, if somewhat too timidly. His Lordship said, "A strong feeling of dissatisfaction as to our system of popular education was now prevalent. The scheme for a purely secular and compulsory education would meet with many obstacles; and it would perhaps be thought safer to extend our present system, and to apply a gentle pressure by requiring certificates of proficiency and attendance before a child was permitted to work for hire." This is good, and fully accords with Mr. Gladstone's enunciation. Once demand "certificates of proficiency," compulsion must soon follow. The Bishop concludes this part of his pastoral with the judicious remark that, "Religious education was that which the clergy must promote," and I would add, the ministers of all denominations; for merely secular instruction would only raise up a Godless community. I cannot conclude these remarks better than by quoting a few words by the Hon. G. Denman, who strongly urges the only other reason I wished to adduce. He says, "What about the future? Something he thought should be done to put down the intoxication which disgraced this civilized land, and the consequent crime and immorality which prevailed. The great question of education also demanded attention. It was disgraceful that in a rich and powerful community like that of England, more had not been done to ensure the attainment of the rudiments of a sound and useful education by every person not an idiot or a lunatic. To the disappointment of Mr. Lowe, and to his (Mr. Denman's) great delight the compulsory education of the poor had become an absolute necessity. Mr. Lowe had at last made the great admission, that as

Slater Street Board School, built 1874 - one of the first Board Schools in Leicester - still standing

long as you kept the working classes out of the franchise, it was possible to leave them ignorant of their danger. Now that the working class had power, they must be educated in order to diminish that danger. Such was the admission of Mr. Lowe. Was there ever a stronger argument in favour of progression - progression in order to obtain a good moral and religious people? No man in his senses would deny that education produced goodness, morality, and religion more than any other agency that existed." These are hopeful utterances, and now that our orthodox brethren no longer startle at the idea of "state aid," and our Mialls and Baineses admit that voluntaryism is inadequate to the requirements of education, it may be safely concluded that the question will make way.[5]

The educational implications of the new Workshops' Regulation Act were consequently commended by Dare in 1868:

This Act is a well meant piece of legislation. It must effect some good, as it bears directly upon a portion of the most neglected children. The Town Clerk, S. Stone, Esq., prepared a very ample and intelligible digest of the Act, which was posted throughout the borough, and the Council authorized certain officers to enforce its observations as far as possible. I learn from the inspector, Mr. Wright, that "there are now 583 children attending schools consequent upon the adoption of the Workshop Act." Of these our day school has the greatest number attending it of any single school in the town. The British School admits only those who had been pupils there before going to work, so that scarcely any attend under the new Act. The more respectable employers comply with the system, and I know some who discharged all whose ages came under its regulations. It will be found that the Act is chiefly evaded by small unprincipled employers, and needy, ignorant, or drunken parents. A sharp eye must be kept on "Finishers," who carry on their business in private houses, - on children who "go on errands," and on parents, who, idle and ignorant themselves, care nothing about the moral condition of their poor neglected little ones. However, though six hundred children at school half their time is but a small number rescued from the 7000 in the town, who are receiving no instruction, it is doing something.[6]

By 1875, Dare was acknowledging the efforts of the local School Board - established under the 1870 Education Act - in providing new Board Schools and in appointing school visitors to enforce attendance following the introduction of compulsion bye-laws in 1874. Yet problems are still detected:

Considering the short time the Board Schools have been in operation in this town, and the kind of children and parents they have had to take in hand, there is a marked difference in their respective localities; the children roaming at will, annoying passers-by, and learning all manner of vicious and ineradicable habits are much fewer in number. Till recently, such children were never seen with a book or slate in their possession, but now, instead of playing in the gutter, or handling some dangerous play-thing, many may be seen conning their lessons, or trying to write some words or figures on their slates, and withal, with cleaner faces and better behaviour as they pass along the streets.

The greatest difficulty that our School Board will have to encounter will be in relation to the half-timers, and those pitiable young roughs, who have hitherto been under no parental control, and who have nearly passed school age. Many of these, like fish from the net, will slip from its

Wyggeston's Boys' Grammar School, Highcross Street, opened 1877 - Leicester Grammar School today

power. A great number of them are employed and concealed in the numerous and obscure "Nail-up" and "Finishing" shops. Here they are kept from school by all manner of subterfuges, and demoralized by the degraded men, who work them at the most unreasonable hours. As their engagements are of short duration, they soon earn considerable wages of which they retain the greater portion for themselves; and quickly breaking loose from all restraint, they soon acquire the vicious habits, and rush into the disgusting animalism of their older compeers, and thus rise up to swell the ranks of crime and immorality, instead of becoming useful and happy members of society. The penalty for employing children who ought to be "full-timers" at school must be invariably exacted, and universal compulsion, which Mr. Cross has now virtually given us, must be enforced, except in very peculiar cases, which common humanity would be sure to discover.

At present the various plans of the School Boards are necessarily in a great measure tentative. They must be modified by "My Lords," in accordance with the suggestions of growing experience, and the Government having shortened the hours of labour, it is to be hoped that all Board Schools will be opened for elementary instruction after factory hours, through the whole of the winter.[7]

By his last *Report* in 1876, the tone is decidedly optimistic, particular attention being drawn to the setting up of Wigston's Grammar School with its Huxleyian aim of providing an educational ladder for bright working-class children. Making a comparison with the educational situation of working-class children in 1851, Dare states:

More than two thirds of the children attended no school, now nearly the whole attend. The common Day Schools have more than doubled, and what is of greater importance to the once neglected children there are now seven Board Schools in active operation, and two more are being built, which, if allowed to produce their legitimate influences, must prove of incalculable benefit to the coming generation. A certain number, too, of working men's children will be admitted by examination to Wigston's New Grammar School, so that the lowliest child, if he have ability, will have a career opened to him that may lead to the highest seats of learning or science. Our Discussion Class put themselves into communication with the Commissioners of Endowed Schools, &c., praying them to enlarge the number to be admitted. Their Lordships commended the tone of the petition, and granted its prayer.[8]

The Reverend James Went, M.A., headmaster of the Wyggeston's Boys' Grammar School, 1877-1919

Recreation

Dare regarded recreational activity as an important index of the general well-being of the population. Throughout his *Reports* he regularly drew attention to what he considered to be highly questionable working-class relaxations. A whole range came under fire: dog-fighting, pigeon-flying, rat-hunting and the rat-pit, the races, fairs, swimming nude and general frivolous activity in Abbey Meadows, gambling, betting, dancing, bare-fist fighting, street fighting. The issue which attracted his gravest concern, however, was drinking. He often referred to the craving for drink which gripped and destroyed many of the working classes. He describes instances of it in 1850:

D., a father and two daughters (one fourteen and the other twelve years of age), occupy but one sleeping room, with a heap of rubbish for a bed on the floor. The wife is in a distant town, living on the wages of infamy; the father is intoxicated as often as he can get the means. He makes these poor girls earn him money by seaming, keeping them at work till midnight, and making them get up at three or four o'clock to begin again. He pawns every article of clothing, if at any time they manage to obtain a garment by extra exertions. It would be a blessing if children so situated could be rescued from their own parents. B., is another wretched household. The father is a confirmed drunkard, and consequently want and misery have taken their abode under his roof. The wife looks half-starved; the children slip about in filthy rags; the only furniture is a small broken table, and a chair or two in the same condition. When the thirst for strong drink rages, everything that can be pawned is pledged for its gratification. While this is the case, there is no hope of elevation. Benevolence only increases the means of gratifying the depraved appetite.[1]

The work of the Leicester Temperance Society in dealing with the drink problem was early on praised by Dare:

Having been requested, at the last annual meeting of this society, to serve on its Committee, during the current year, I consented with pleasure to the appointment. I considered the nomination a proof of enlarged sympathy for the poor - for the miserable drunkard. I attended nearly the whole of the meetings and rejoice to bear testimony to the good the society is effecting. Excessive drinking is one of the crying evils here, as it is in all our large towns. Many drunkards have been reclaimed. I meet several in my own visits. It is very pleasing to see the change that has been produced in themselves and their families. Three-legged tables and bottomless chairs have been removed by "mahogany snaps" or "Windsors" glittering with French polish. The wife and the child have forgotten their squalor and misery in returning health and cheerfulness, whilst the husband spends his evenings at his own fireside, or having thrown aside his filthy habiliments, is foremost in the lecture-room, and regular at the temple of worship. One of the best features of the society is that it calls into living co-operation individuals of all sects and parties and social status. It is gratifying to refer to these signs of enlightenment and liberality. They must tend to enhance its usefulness and success.

A Temperance Hall is about to be erected, to enable the Committee to complete the various machinery of the society, which, in addition to

Mr Tarry's rat-pit on Soar Lane in the 1870s - a popular 'sport' in the period

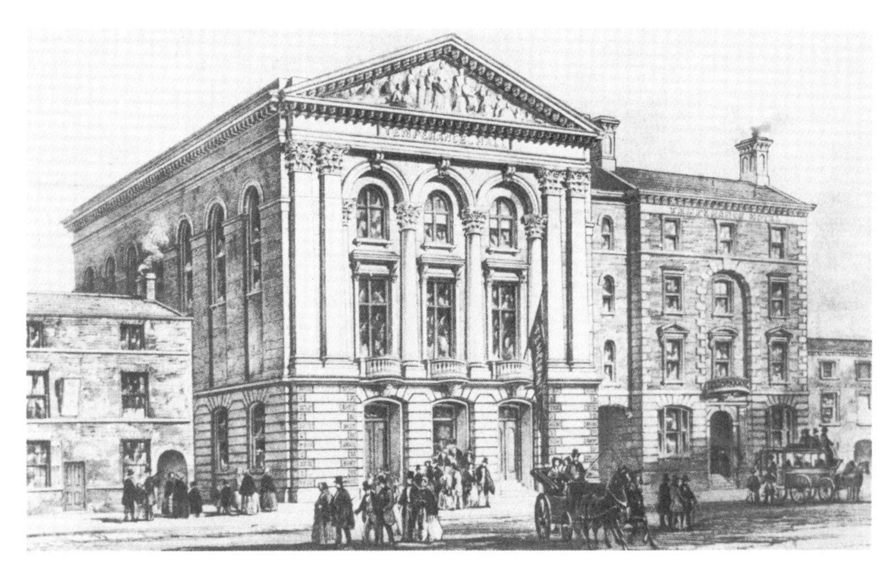

The Temperance Hall, Granby Street, 1857

its present operations, will comprehend an organized system of visiting, juvenile classes, instructional branches, and reading rooms. This institution is deserving of universal support.[2]

Dare placed great emphasis on the need to provide rational recreations as counter-attractions to questionable relaxations like drinking. Outdoor as well as indoor activities had to be provided. Recurringly in his early *Reports*, however, Dare was critical of moral agencies, like the Temperance Society, for their failure to provide sufficient, free counter-attractions for the really neglected:

Neglected! asks the Temperance advocate. Turn him over to me; let me take him under hand. And he does take him in hand, and knocks the pot and the pipe from his grasp; but he neither substitutes any other hobby, nor instructs his mind; consequently he is deterred from taking the pledge, or relapses after having signed. In many cases, too, as I have been credibly informed, his abstinence costs more than his drunkenness, through gambling and indulgence in what are called "Temperance drinks" till late hours at coffee shops, to say nothing of the necessary contributions for the support of the cause.

In all movements where payments are required, voluntaryism fails to produce its ultimate benefits. For, as this principle demands pecuniary as well as other co-operation, the needy are excluded. Again, the social tea-gatherings and rural fêtes, now become so fashionable, and such powerful agencies in the work of moral progress, are all beyond the means of the "poor and lowly." The same remark will apply to every kind of better amusement. They are shut out from the "legitimate-drama," the concert, and the lecture; consequently they rush to the monstrosities of the strolling player or the more horrid orgies of the back room of the low tavern.[3]

Dare was still making the same criticisms in the 1860s. In 1864, for instance, he pointed out that moral agencies only reached 'those who already possess some little taste and information'.[4] In 1868, he urged the Half-Day Holiday Movement in the town to provide more in the way of free rational recreations:

Of the half-holiday movement I would say that if it is to be an institution, it had better be universal, so that sports and amusements may be organized for it, similar to those of the Athletic Society. Some might be borrowed from our Scotch neighbours, and even from the old Greeks, who wisely made their games and pastimes instrumental in developing their beautiful human forms, and ultimately their unsurpassable sculptures. Workmen might then agree to be fined for leaving their occupations at any other time, as by doing so at uncertain intervals they hinder numbers who can only carry on their labours in conjunction with them. In the winter, lectures might be given bearing on our local handicrafts, on sanitary, literary, and various other subjects. Organizations for holidays and relaxations are one of the pressing wants of the age, for there are scarcely any resorts where the toilers may spend their leisure hours, except the low ale house, detestable wine shops, or demoralizing music halls. As there is so much musical talent in the town, and such a general love for music, why could not our native performers unite and present some of the popular oratorios through the winter, at nominal prices. The audiences contemplated would not require the extravagantly high paid artists from a distance. I am sure such performances would afford immense delight, and powerfully tend to correct the vicious taste created by "bones" and the banjo. No doubt many who have the means would render pecuniary assistance. Excursions are good, but they are expensive and not applicable all the year. All recreations for the poor should be provided with little or no expense.[5]

Thomas Cook: key figure in the local Temperance movement and rational recreationist - pioneer of the excursion trip

Despite these criticisms, however, it seems clear that much was done in the local community to provide rational indoor and outdoor recreations for the working classes during the period. Dare acknowledged the fact in his regular references to these provisions.

In 1846 he drew attention to the local Allotment movement:

The Allotment-system is highly appreciated by many of the operatives, and I have frequently been asked whether more land could not be procured for this purpose? I am told an additional portion in the neighbourhood of "the North" would be thankfully received by numbers of workmen in that locality. From experience, long and extensive, I consider this system a means of bettering the poor man. If he be careful not to take more land than he can dig, and stock himself, it will generally prove a source of amusement, health, and profit.[6]

Dare also praised the excursions, rural fêtes and brass bands being increasingly organised by local employers for their workers. Factory treats were particularly important, in Dare's view, since the mingling of masters and men softened class differences. By 1859, he was reporting:

Glancing over the years that I have been in this town, it is very apparent that a better feeling has gradually arisen between all the larger employers and their workpeople. Many I know are anxious in seasons of depression to soften the more rigid principles of political economy, by Christian kindness and liberality in the conduct of their establishments. And the annual reunions in excursions, rural fêtes, and other social enjoyments that have now become one of the "facts" of the times, are an important means of supplying those kinds of recreation that the "age of great cities" so much requires. A day spent in a trip to the romantic scenery of some distant locality; the rural gathering at Bradgate, Bardon, or in the beautiful seclusion of the home park, where the various classes mingle "a-dancing on the green," at once recalls the olden times of "merrie England," and awakens pleasures and memories that lighten many an hour of toil and become extinguished only with life itself. Several of the factories have now brass bands formed amongst their own workpeople, to be ready with music at their social meetings, and others are following their example.[7]

In 1864 he reported on one firm's outing that he had personally attended:

I had the pleasure in the summer of spending a day with the hands of a very large establishment. The locality chosen for the holiday was Kenilworth. The heads of the firm accompanied their hands, numbering about five hundred, together with several friends who were specially invited to join them, with the view of diffusing a feeling of kindness and hilarity amongst them. They sat at tea, mingled in the country dance, or rambled over the magnificent ruins together, as "fancy or will determined," the employers or visitors referring to the various interesting legends or historical associations connected with them for the information and amusement of the merry groups. All enjoyed themselves without restraint, neither quarrel nor drunkenness disgraced the scene, and the whole of the hands were at work the next morning at the usual time. Unless such gatherings generally are conducted in a similar spirit, they are a positive evil, little better than the saturnalia of the pothouse or singing room, and only increase instead of diminishing the vicious influences already at work in society. There requires, too, more friendly intercourse amongst the different sections of the community. Judge Talfourd's last and dying words should be written in gold over the altar of every temple, "More sympathy between the rich and the poor!" From the hurrying and driving in the fierce battle of life - the wealthy to maintain their position, and the poor to snatch the necessaries of existence, - or worse, from selfishness and indulgence, men become insulated and alienated from each other, and the higher claims of humanity and the immortal soul are forgotten.[8]

Organised cricket on Victoria Park, 1870s

Dare also commended the efforts made to provide recreation grounds and parks. In 1866, for instance, he noted:

Further steps have been wisely taken to make the race-course more subservient to sanitary and recreative purposes. It is now appropriately named Victoria Park, a fine promenade - to be extended - has been opened, bordered with rows of "bee-loving lindens," and a handsome pavilion has been built in room of the old unsightly stand, and, what is of more importance, to afford accommodation for social, musical, and other gatherings of an elevating tendency, before which dissipation and rowdyism will, we trust, to a great extent disappear. The resident park keeper will secure better order amongst the juvenile promenaders. As the old Cricket Ground is now wholly covered with houses, could not a "strip of green" be preserved for "the little ones," somewhere in the neighbourhood of the Willow Bridge?[9]

By 1868, Victoria Park was being used for organised cricket and an Agricultural and Horticultural Show - the forerunner of the modern City of Leicester Show:

The admission of cricketers to Victoria Park, and the opening of recreation grounds on the Welford-road and at the West end are essential privileges for the working classes, promotive of health and harmless enjoyment, and relieving the pasture from over-crowding. Another pleasing feature of the year was the Agricultural and Horticultural Show. It furnished a most gratifying and instructive holiday to the classes. The corporation spared no efforts to meet its necessary requirements. Spectators were delighted with the beautiful floral productions - the wonderful animals, and the novel and powerful implements, that tend so much to diminish drudgery and subdue the elements to the service of man. Surely our Hunts and Pickerings, our Howards and Fowlers, are amongst the true heroes and civilizers of humanity.

A taste for botany diffused amongst the workers would tend a little to diminish depredations in the fields, and do away with some of the disgusting gatherings on Sundays at the outlets of the town, for herbalists are generally inoffensive observers of nature; and why should not Leicester have, like Manchester and other places in the north, its native botanists amongst the toilers, capable of directing the scientific stranger, who comes to enquire about the numerous and beautiful flora of the county? Victoria Park was admirably adapted for the Show, and the town, with its triumphal arches and illuminations, assumed a very pleasing appearance, making every one, as it were, a part of the gala, and securing universal satisfaction.[10]

Nude bathing in the Soar, Abbey Meadows - condemned by middle-class respectability in the period

Boating on the Soar - a popular pastime from the 1870s

In 1876, Dare noted further:

In addition to the Racecourse, several recreation grounds have been opened on different sides of the town. It has afforded me very great pleasure to see the active youths and poor little children playing upon the one in view of my residence, and mothers sitting on the grass sewing, with their babes in their laps. The gymnastic apparatus, too, delighted the youngsters, and one novel, if not unique feature, was exhibited in the fact that our energetic chief of police visited the recreation grounds in turn with an excellent brass band, whose members all belong to the police force. This is very gratifying and commendable, showing that if at times it is his duty to punish, he is willing to please.[11]

Dare also praised the proposals in hand in the 1870s to improve bathing facilities in the town:

I have heard, and hope the report is true, that the Corporation have determined to erect commodious baths for the toilers in our shops and factories. The town, hitherto, has not been very well provided with bathing places. With the exception of one retired spot on the river, and the public bath on the New Walk, there are no proper places set apart for this healthful exercise, so necessary in large manufacturing towns. The bathing place in the Pasture is too much exposed, or at any rate should be better superintended. I have seen fellows splashing about up to the North Bridge in full view of the public road and contiguous factories; and other like disgusting exhibitions at the top of Soar Lane coal wharf, and near the end of my own garden adjoining the new mill, where hundreds are passing to and from their work all day long. Certain classes of roughs can only enjoy themselves by annoying decent people. The bathing in the Pasture also deprives respectable females of the pleasant recreation of boating, and shuts its use on summer evenings from the nurse-girl and adjacent householder. Cannot the alterations necessitated by the Flood Scheme, now being carried out, be utilised by turning them into a promenade along the margin of the river, shaded with odorous limes, and thus dedicated to health and enjoyment, preserve it from its present repulsive desecration? There should be open-air concerts here on summer evenings as well as on the Racecourse. I call the attention of working men's bands to this subject against another season. But what I wish more particularly to point out in reference to the previous subject is, that during another year there has been absolutely no opportunity for the female factory workers to bathe. The time set apart for them at the New Walk was working time, in the morning, when it was impossible for them to attend. Now, what is wanted is, that, at least, two whole evenings each week should be reserved for the female operatives to bathe after working hours.[12]

Rational indoor recreations were also provided in the period. Dare reported several in 1864:

It is gratifying to notice the efforts made during the last winter to provide for the amusement of the neglected classes. The Museum was opened with gaslight, and an excellent course of lectures, explanatory of the objects it contains, was delivered gratuitously by competent lecturers, which we know were highly appreciated by the numerous workers who attended. The Mechanics' Institute also gave a very efficient course of Penny Readings, interspersed with classical music. The Great Meeting Sunday School, and I believe some others, opened amusement classes on week-day evenings to which the parents of children were kindly and judiciously invited. Penny Readings too and Literary and Musical Entertainments were given by some of the orthodox bodies, either in their school-rooms or chapels.

I have learnt with satisfaction that in several parts of the town "Mothers' Meetings" have been established and are doing much good in implanting better ideas of domestic management, and in inducing members of families to attend places of worship. I earnestly hope that the ladies of our denomination will be induced to open a Mothers' Meeting, as the surest way to find access to the hearts of the poor is to enter with them upon some practical and useful work. Many an idle and drinking husband has been won back to temperance and industry by the improved habits of those dependent upon him.[13]

Dare regarded reading as an important indoor pastime and in 1850, anxious to ascertain the reading tastes of the working classes, he undertook a survey of the average circulation of weekly penny publications in the town. The same report drew attention to the poor quality engravings found in working-class homes, portraying highly dubious characters:

Of Lloyd's works there are 765, and of Reynolds's 563, taken weekly. These consist almost wholly of tales of the "Newgate Calendar class," as one of the sellers styled them - pandering to the grossest passions of uneducated minds. Their vicious tendency may be inferred from their titles: "Paul Clifford, or Hurrah for the Road!" "Claude Du Val," "Ella the Outcast," and "The Mysteries of the Court of London," are amongst the number. The last-mentioned is, I am informed, the worst of its kind. It is somewhat curious that the purlieus of royalty should furnish the materials for pandering to the sensualism of the uninstructed. Extremes meet. It seems to be the same vitiated taste that seeks the loose novel in polished society, as that which leads the vulgar to devour the exciting trash just mentioned. Some minds delight in fiction. The labour of thinking is too much for them. A portion of such minds are found in every rank of life. Of the London Journal there are 588 taken weekly. This, I am told by an intelligent agent, is the best serial of its class, and took the lead in "improving the moral tone of the weekly quarto size, introducing facts, scientific paragraphs, domestic economies, &c." The People, by Joseph Barker, about a dozen copies. The Reasoner, 60: in this work Atheism is boldly avowed. It is conducted in a candid and earnest manner. Miscellaneous sceptical works, such as Free-thinker's Magazine, about 80. The Red Republican, edited by Harney, 66. National Instructor, by O'Connor, 76. Cooper's Journal, about 150 at the time of its recent suspension. Song books, 100. Sunday

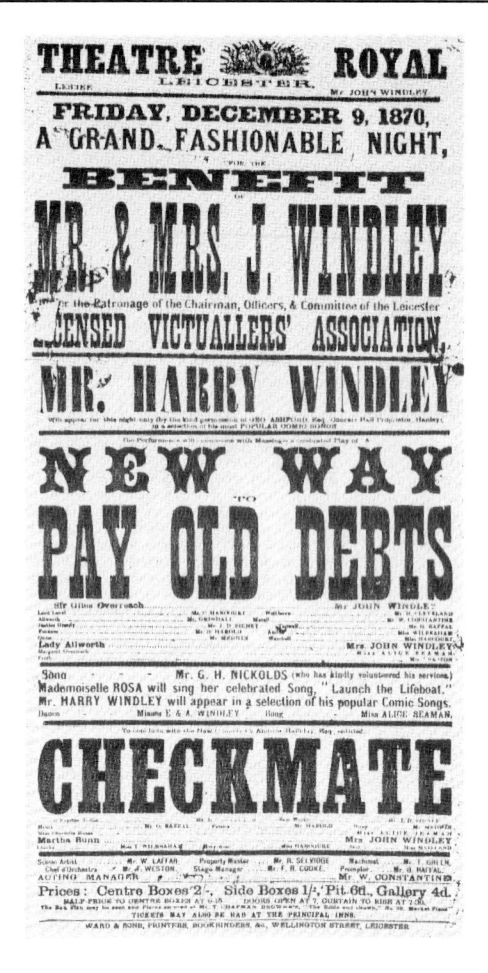

Theatre Royal, Leicester, playbill from 1870

Times, 12: this sheet is nearly superseded by Lloyd's penny tales, and by some agents its issue was returned with these. Tales of improved character published by Willoughby, such as William Tell, &c., about 350. Penny Illustrated News, 30. News of the World, 570. Weekly Times, 150. Lloyd's News, 140; and Reynolds' News, about 100. These last four are cheap stamped papers, and consist principally of compilations from the daily papers, leaning, of course, in politics, to the ultra side of liberalism. Of the Family Herald, 532 copies are taken weekly. This is a useful work, coming between the "trash" and others of a still higher quality. Working Man's Friend, 206. Chambers' Papers for the People, 61. Knight's Half-hours, 50. Family Friend, 320. The Public Good, 26. Cottage Gardener, 24. Household Words, 101. Chambers' Journal, 102. Chambers' Information for the People, 20. Hogg's Instructor, 20. Eliza Cook's Journal, 50. Family Economist, 155. Home Circle, 60. People and Howitt's Journal, 21. Miscellaneous penny tales of healthful tone, not mentioned above, 30.

From these figures it will be seen that there are considerably more than 6000 copies of penny publications taken weekly in this town. As far as I can judge, about a third of this circulation is of decidedly immoral tendency. But from

Interior of the Free Library c.1880

various inquiries, my impressions as to the reading taste of the working classes are, upon the whole, of a favourable character. One intelligent agent gave it as his judgement, that a portion of the most exceptionable works go amongst the middle and upper classes, and that it is only because the working class is the largest, that it seems to take the greatest number. Another very intelligent publisher informed me that frequently readers would begin with the lowest kind of tales, and in a while ask for works of a better description.

There is now a multiplicity of cheap works issuing daily from the press upon almost every subject. It would be impossible barely to enumerate them. Walkingame's Arithmetic, complete, and Dr. Mavor's Old Standard Spelling-book, may now be each had for fourpence. Maps, too, are issued at a penny each. And a yet more hopeful sign is, that such writers as Cockton, Albert Smith, &c., are issuing an improved class of penny tales. These will, in a great measure, supersede the exciting trash of the day.

Penny Religious Literature taken in the town: this, I believe, is nearly all issued monthly. Of cheap religious publications, varying from one halfpenny to threepence monthly - (very few of the latter) - nearly 4000 are issued. These go principally into the Sunday Schools, and are therefore spread amongst the working classes. Of high Calvinistic works there are about 220 issued monthly. A few of these are twopence each. Some of their titles are curious, such as "The Vessel," "The Casket," "The Trumpet," and "The Wrestler."

There sadly wants a better kind of engraving for the decoration of the dwellings of the poor. The walls are bedizened now, in numberless instances, with representations of prize-fighters, banditti, notorious highwaymen, or mysterious ruffians, muffled in cloaks, with a brace or two of pistols in their belts, and a long naked dirk flourishing in the air, hurrying along to do "a deed without a name." Such pictures perpetually before the eye cannot but have a bad influence. These silent actors of atrocities must brutalize the feelings of those who are constantly seeing them. I have noticed in my rounds but few appropriate prints for cottages. One was a cheerful pleasing representation of the "Four Seasons." Here, then, is an ample field for improving the taste of the working classes. They are fond of pictures, and since the improvement of trade, hundreds of cottages have been ornamented with such engravings as have been accessible. No doubt, in many cases, had better been in the market, they would have been preferred. Let our Cruikshanks and Kenny Meadows meet the demand. The success of "The Bottle" shows that true art is appreciated by the cottager. The porcelain ornaments, too, for the mantel-piece, might be much improved in design, and thus be made a powerful means of refining the general taste. There is a profusion of these as well as of pictures amongst many of the poor. They are indications of cultivable minds. Objective beauty is the symbolism of the spiritual nature of man, and gradually leads him to the possession and enjoyment of subjective beauty. And as soon as an individual reverences his intellectual and higher powers, he is lifted from all grosser defilements.[14]

In 1873, Dare drew attention to the service provided by the Free Library:

It is equally gratifying to see volumes from the Free Library in so many working men's cottages. Chatting one day with a very intelligent young man as to the working of the Free Library, and the character of the works it contains, I found that he was most interested in the reference department, and he thought many readers would feel it a great boon if they could have some of the works to study at home. As it must be the desire of the benelovent and liberal minded founders to make it as useful as possible, I pressed him to give me his views upon the subject. He writes: "It has always seemed to me to be a pity that so large a proportion of the Free Library should be put in the reference department. That department is the proper place for Lexicons, Encyclopaedias, Dictionaries of all descriptions, and all books which are strictly works of reference, but it contains also a great number of works which have no business whatever in a reference department. Such for instance are the following, which I select as being in accordance with my own special tastes: Malthus on Population, Leckey's History of Rationalism in Europe, Lubbock's Pre-Historic Times, Hobbes's Works, Max Muller's Lectures on the Science of Language and Chips from a German Workshop, Alex. Bains' Logic, Mental and Moral Science, and Senses and the Intellect, Sir W. Hamilton's Discussions on Philosophy, and Lectures on

Spring and Autumn Fairs were regular events. This one was on Humberstone Gate in the 1890s

Metaphysics and Logic, J. S. Mill's Auguste Comte and Positivism, Dissertations and Discussions, and Examination of Sir W. Hamilton's Philosophy. To place such books as these in the reference department seems to me to be rendering them entirely useless. If any one wishes to master them, it will not be sufficient to take them up at distant intervals, and read a little now and a little then; he must devote to them a persistent course of reading and who can be expected to divorce himself from his own fireside and family night after night, for weeks, which would be necessary in order to accomplish his purpose? And why should they, whose tastes lie in the direction of such literature, be denied the privilege accorded to the readers of fiction - of taking it to their own homes. It seems to me that such tastes should be encouraged rather than having obstacles placed in the way of their gratification. It can scarcely be said that these books are too expensive to be placed in the lending department, for there are many in that department a great deal more expensive. Grote's History of Greece, for instance, is £3. 12s., while of those which I have quoted, four are 16s., one 15s., two 10s. 6d., and one 6s.; and it should be borne in mind that readers of such books are not a class of persons likely to ill-use them. There is another matter which deserves mention, that is, the curious fact that no more than seven days are allowed for the perusal of any book, whatever may be its magnitude. It may be renewed, it is true, but why not allow a reasonable time for its reading, and save this unnecessary trouble both to the librarian and the borrower? I have frequently had to wait at the Library a quarter-of-an-hour or twenty minutes and there is no reason why I should have to do this two or three times when once would do."[15]

By 1876, Dare was commending the efforts of religious bodies in providing rational recreations:

It is satisfactory to know that most of the religious bodies have now wisely added some kind of amusement or recreation for the young, more especially, to their other praiseworthy efforts. We can remember the time when to talk of singing Handel's choruses, giving a popular lecture, or holding a penny concert in connection with religious agencies, would have been thought quite profane; so, as children grew up, many of them, led by a natural craving, sought relaxation in questionable company. That time has happily passed away, and various facilities for the improvement and enjoyment of life have vastly increased with the general advancement of the town.[16]

Despite the efforts of the rational recreation movement in Leicester, however, Dare nevertheless recognised that many of the working classes remained untouched by them. Disreputable amusements often appeared to Dare to be proliferating rather than declining. In 1864, for instance, he drew attention to the abject behaviour associated with many firms' summer outings:

The manner in which many of the larger gatherings of workmen for a rural holiday manage what they call their recreations, reflects little credit either on their taste or judgement. Often the fête ends in a mere riotous debauch, or is continued in the town for many days, to the neglect of employment, self-degradation, and the privation of helpless dependents.

From the unmanly and reckless conduct of

many of these assemblages, in chasing the deer, breaking trees, disturbing the game and fish, or fighting amongst themselves, access to the beautiful park at Bradgate has been restricted to only one day in the week during the season for out-door relaxations. "I saw," says Swedenborg, "a beautiful truth let down from heaven into hell, and there it became a lie." And thus do these poor men unconsciously turn the blessings they might enjoy into curses, polluting the air with blasphemy, and staining the great earth with their blood. Nor are these open-air revels the worst features in these holidays; it is the after consequences that are the most deplorable. An extensive and benevolent employer, who is most anxious for the welfare and improvement of the working classes, informs me that such a holiday, instead of invigorating and increasing the health of his hands, renders them unfit to resume their work in due time, and consequently they suffer a loss in money spent, work neglected, and wages unearned, of not less than three hundred pounds. It is a lamentable fact that, unless parties who have some moral control over the men accompany them, these holidays of great gatherings exercise a pernicious rather than a beneficial influence.[17]

Dare also detected a marked increase in betting and gambling amongst Leicester's working classes:

Whether from the fact that many of the old pastimes have been suppressed, or from the concentration of greater numbers of working men in certain occupations, the passion for "betting and gambling" amongst them seems on the increase. Art Unions, and bazaars, conducted on the same principles, for charitable, and even religious purposes, such as building schools, chapels and churches, no doubt tend to foster this pernicious habit. I have now before me the prospectus of "a drawing on the plan of the Art Union," in which are offered three nice cottages, gold and silver watches, a piano, and various other valuable articles, including a wedding dress and gold ring, to be selected from any shop in London, and "a pig born last February, now fattening for the purpose, a perfect beauty!" The proceeds of this Bazaar are in aid of "Poor Schools and a new church," all, of course under the directions of clergymen. I see too, in the Standard newspaper there is a running advertisement of a similar lottery under the auspices of Magistrates, Aldermen and other notabilities, to come off at Southampton for the benefit of a widow lady. It is headed, "Four houses, one shilling each," meaning thereby the price of the tickets. In the former lottery they are sixpence each. Now, are not such transactions direct appeals to the gambling propensities of the masses? But no doubt the vast increase of "horse-racing revels," tends, more than any other cause to develop and strengthen this feeling in all classes of society. "Books" are made up and Sweepstakes subscribed to, in all parts of the country, referring to races, never witnessed by the bettors themselves, but who, from the sporting papers are as familiar with the names and qualities of the various horses as the noble owners themselves, and speculate with the same morbid excitement upon the chances of the turf. In referring to this growing practice of betting and gambling, a writer in the Spectator, who is reviewing an excellent work on the progress of the working classes, remarks, when speaking of the Sporting Press: "It was not long ago that Bell's Life was almost the only representative of the class. Within a very few years nearly a score of competitors have sprung up, of which upwards of a dozen, some of them appearing twice or three times a week, seem to have attained a paying, and in some instances a very profitable circulation. To this result, the popularity of horse-racing and other forms of sport among the working classes has, without doubt, very materially contributed. Let it be added too, that no morning or evening 'daily' would be complete without its regular column of sporting

Leicester races on Victoria Park, 1870s

intelligence."

As the race-course belongs to the Corporation, why could not the Council prohibit "rouge-et-noire," and numerous other games of chance and gambling practices. An intelligent observer who is friendly to every proper amusement, informs me that the game of throwing at cocoa nuts is carried on chiefly by loose females, whose obscene inuendoes cannot but corrupt the thoughtless youths who are induced to hazard a throw. All manner of filthy allusions are continually made use of to lead them on to join in the game. They catch them, and repeat them, and turn away laughing at their enlarged vocabulary of slang and obscenity.[18]

In 1865 Dare referred to an increase in a wide range of immoral working-class pursuits. Yet it was the apparent increase in working-class drinking that caused him most anxiety. To add substance to his concern, Dare provides a vivid description of the activities inside Leicester's new and larger singing-drinking saloons, bringing alive the central role drink played in working-class life. The report has additional significance in its demonstration of how children were readily socialised into drink and vice as a way of life:

I requested an intelligent working man, who is well acquainted with the views and habits of his order, to furnish me with his impression as to the causes of their condition. After alluding to the money and labour spent upon their education, and other means for their improvement, with such poor results, he proceeds:

"It is the duty of every right-thinking man to ascertain, as far as possible, why the results are so small compared with the efforts put forth. That the children of the present generation are less apt in learning cannot be the cause, for we meet with precocity on every side. Of course the primary cause is the want of more lengthened education and moral training. Another chief cause I take to be the change which has taken place during the last few years in the modes of employment, and the facility it has given to the youth of our town for earning money. This enables them too soon to become 'independent,' and hence they form a determination too early in life to throw off all parental control. Another reason is the present mode of the division of labour, which makes it necessary that both girls and boys should be constantly in the same rooms with the adults of their respective sex, who speak and act as though the young were not present. The consequence is, they become early in life familiar with scenes of immorality, crime, and every phase of our social vices, as their ears are not spared the grossest obscenity, and actions and over-night's adventures are often described before them that would make a demon blush. Thus the passions are goaded, manhood and womanhood are ante-dated, and a vast amount

A 'Free-and-Easy' as seen by the Temperance Society, c.1880

of youthful iniquity and crime is the consequence. Another cause may be found in the introduction of the Casino and common singing rooms into our populous towns; for no sooner is it known that the working classes are earning good wages than speculators are sure to find out that these establishments are needed. Immediately they are opened, hundreds flock to them from the public-houses and the home-fireside, and more drink is consumed than ever. Many individuals, particularly females who consider themselves above the society of the common tap room or ginshop, see no harm in visiting these places, but where they come in contact with the same or even worse company. For while the general gatherings at the beershops are chiefly the improvident and drunken of our male population, and occasionally their wives who have gone to get them home, and who are often in this manner led into the same habits, and which is the cause, in many instances, of slatternly wives and dirty husbands, at the other place they come into contact not only with young men, who would induce them to drink, and persuade them to stay out late at nights, but also with young women who were perhaps a few months ago, what they are now, - pure, but giddy and thoughtless; but having now become lost to all sense of decency, and retaliating on society by helping to swell the numbers of the profligate and immoral who infest the town. I have visited these places, and therefore speak from experience. One Friday evening I went to one of our large singing saloons. It is capable of seating about six hundred persons, who are admitted by ticket marked 2d., 4d., or 6d., according as purchasers wished to go to the back or front seats on the floor, or to the gallery. The room is well decorated, and tolerably clean. The seats are the same kind as those used at the Temperance Hall with backs to them, with this addition - at the back of each is fastened a kind of spout, which the company use to put their bottles and glasses upon. I was scarcely seated before a fussy waiter - of whom there are a great many constantly in the room - came to know my orders. All are expected to drink. The females generally seemed to prefer spirituous liquors. The ages of those present ranged apparently from sixteen to seventy. Many who were mothers had their infants with them. I noticed in particular a young woman about five and twenty years of age, who came with two little children, seemingly all her family, - one at the breast, the other rather more than two years old. She was a decently dressed, cleanly little woman, and appeared to have locked up the house to come, for she had the key of the door on her finger. She seemed at once quite at home, standing the eldest child on the seat to see the performance, while she nursed the other, and let them both drink out of her glass. About nine o'clock the audience began to muster pretty strong, and there was a sprinkling of every class, from the shoe-finishers 'sweaters' to the tradesman and professional gentleman. The arrangements for the performers are the same as at the theatre, with the music in front of the stage. If there is the slightest applause, the conductor rises again and calls out that Mr. or Mrs. will sing again. These repetitions are apparently to eke out the performance and afford time for drinking, for the singer re-appears but slowly, while the waiters hurry around for orders, in which they are always pretty successful. I noticed on this night that a very large proportion of those present belonged to some of those firms in the shoe-trade, who pay on Friday, and who were spending a day sooner merely because they had the money, and could not keep it. The performances consist generally of three-sixths of the nigger element, two-sixths comic, and one-sixth sentimental. The comic pieces appear to be the greatest favourites, if sufficiently indecent, or containing enough of what the French call 'double entendre:' then they will applaud and encore without mercy. Some time since, another place for similar entertainments was opened, with a list of prices to the back and front seats, and also to the snug. Now I never thoroughly understood what this compartment was. I went another time, on a Saturday night, when the whole place was dreadfully crowded. We had some minutes to wait before we could pass in. During that time about sixty passed out; and while passing, or rather squeezing upstairs, numbers were squeezing in the opposite direction, in the midst of which an altercation occurred. A boy about sixteen was trying to gain admittance, but was refused, though he had a cheque, which he said he had received a short time previously. The proprietor was called, and he settled the thing at once, by stating that they never admitted any of his age; and from what I saw I believe they do not admit any boys on Saturday nights, for then they can get plenty of men and women. But going on Thursday night, there was an abundance of both boys and girls younger than he present, many of whom were exceedingly ill-behaved; some were in utter rags, but such are not refused admittance in the middle of the week, when less company assembles. I learn that many are admitted free

William Paul, local singing-saloon proprietor, 1870s

on Tuesday, Wednesday, and Thursday nights, for the purpose of securing attendance and profit from the drink consumed. I noticed one very objectionable proceeding. Just inside the entrance there is always a number lounging about to intercept girls going in, and especially about the bar. If a good-looking girl passes in alone, which is not uncommon, some one of the smartly dressed and ring-fingered gents accosts her, and makes her an offer of drink, which if she accepts is often the first step to a downward course. If she refuses in company of that sort, she is sneered at, and seems out of place. If a young man who is inclined to be steady ventures to go he is tormented to drink both by his compeers and the waiters, who are always pressing for orders, and they really do what tradesmen call a pushing business. On Saturday nights, from the passing out and in that is continually going on, not less than a thousand or more visited this single saloon."

It is shocking in turning from the description of such scenes to state, that in justice it must be added that there are a number of other public places of a far more debased and debasing character, where the looser portions of the population resort, and whose orgies may not be described.

Perhaps one of the worst features of the larger saloons is that whole audiences assemble in them night after night, as in a church or chapel, or rather open church, husbands and wives with their children, courting couples, youths of both sexes, mingled up with the utterly depraved, taking their "sensation" ales and spirituous liquors, smoking and listening to so much that is vicious, and all, as matter of course. How destructive must such habits be of domestic virtue and the comforts and enjoyments of the fireside! With such views of life, how can parents become acquainted with its duties, or sustained in its trials and sorrows that must one day fall upon them. Well may the young grow up precocious and fast, - our streets at recurring intervals become pestiferous, - and their "houses be left unto-them desolate." A moment's glance at out-door scenes and the picture will be complete. It was thought by some that our last Report was rather too darkly coloured. Let me then turn to other reliable observations for a description of them. A keen observer who is anxious for the moral and material prosperity of the town remarks that "there is a mass of under-current depravity at work that vitiates and corrupts the very depths of society." This is seen in an increase of petty thieving, of till-robbing, of personal violence, of wife-desertion and illegitimacy, of assaults, depredations, and drunkenness, that exhibit an utter degradation of character. The police business is so extended at the Weekly Sessions that two courts are generally held, and then the proceedings are protracted for hours beyond what they were five or six years ago. The shoemakers, as a class, are amongst the most reckless and depraved of the community. Employers complain that they are heedlessly destructive in their habits as workmen: their chief care is to get off the work and make it pass muster with the overlooker. They have no pride in their calling to strive after excellence and improvement. If they can but over-reach, or "best," as they term it, the parties with whom they are connected, they plume themselves upon their smartness and dishonesty. When from work, the dog and the pipe, the beer-shop and the skittle-alley, are the favourite modes of enjoyment, and public places of recreation are made pestiferous by their disgraceful conduct. The Spinney Hills, the Willow Bridge Fields, and other popular outlets, where the breeze and the sunlight might be enjoyed, are now become really dangerous places for girls and young persons generally, to use as walks. Then what are called "small-gangs" infest the streets in the evening. At midnight they are followed by the frequenters of singing and dancing-rooms, "making night hideous" with their brawls and obscenity.

Beer-houses are shut up at eleven, and there can be no need in this town for any drinking places to be open after midnight. It is the "small hours" that lead to temptation and ruin. But, it is urged, the clubs require accommodation. Ah, well, the clubs are most of them composed of "Odd Fellows," and they, as well as the Foresters, will have to learn that drinking and late hours are a great obstacle to their increase and prosperity. A respectable house-keeper informs me that the lower portion of the Irish who live in the back streets, from the Old Cross downwards, spend the after part of the Sabbath in utter disregard of its sacred character. Pitch-and-toss, drinking and brawling, make the neighbourhood another Donnybrook Fair. Similar scenes are witnessed on the out-skirts of the town from Sunday to Sunday, especially during summer. They are often referred to in my visits.

The 'Cottage House' beerhouse, Bow Street, 1870s

The Abbey Meadow is a very pandemonium of all that is beastly and brutal. Its demoralising scenes draw aside numbers from Sunday School. New Leicester, too, complains of drunkenness and street fights on Sundays; and yet, of course, the public-houses are all closed.[19]

Illicit Sunday drinking at local beerhouses was an increasing problem, to which Dare made special reference in 1867:

I counted last Sunday morning in the short space to our Mission-room, from 50 to 60 men young and old, lounging about the beer-shops; there were probably inside as many more. An intelligent eye-witness says it is the same in all parts of the town, and that nearly everyone of the beershops has its regular drinkers in forbidden hours. The inspection seems to be carried on by making sudden raids, when some half-dozen tapsters are seized and fined, but the drinking still goes on. And while the policemen will take ale at the back doors, during their pretended calls, the law will still be broken. Most of the parties who support the beer-shops by Sunday drinking are heads of households, many of whose families are receiving charity from very kind, but very unthinking and ill advised persons, as the bestowal only enables reckless husbands and fathers to indulge more largely in drunkenness.[20]

It seems clear that Dare did not regard drinking in moderation and respectability as mutually exclusive, however. This is indicated by his praise for the newly opened Working Men's Club in 1866, at which beer drinking was permitted:

The Working Men's Club demands a passing notice, as it promises to realise its design. The secretary has kindly furnished the following account: -

"The Working Men's Club and Institute has been in existence about six months. The average number, exclusive of honorary members, is 424. The management is vested in three trustees, a president, four vice-presidents, and a committee of twenty-four. The finances are satisfactory; the club is making a profit from refreshments supplied, which will shortly clear off the debt remaining upon the furniture. The rooms are found too small, and it is in contemplation to build more commodious premises, including a working men's hall. Beer is supplied on week-days from 11 o'clock till 2, and from 6 till 10.30. A portion of the committee felt alarmed for the respectability and safety of the club when it was decided to introduce beer. But the alarm speedily subsided when the plan had been tried. The experiment thus far has fairly shown that working men may be trusted; there are no restrictions as to quantity, nor have there been any excesses. The committee have endeavoured, as far as possible, to meet the wishes of the members by providing such recreation and amusement as may be agreeable. An extensive list of newspapers and periodicals has been provided, but the majority of the members do not patronize the reading department. The rooms best filled are those for general conversation and popular games. There are classes for singing, instrumental music, and French, and other classes are in contemplation. The largest room is set apart on Monday and Saturday evenings for music and singing, on Wednesday for discussions and lectures, and on Friday for topics of the week. The rooms are open on Sundays from 2 till 10 o'clock, but with the exception of the conversation room in the evening, the attendance during the summer months has been small."

Being myself on its committee, I have occasionally gone to observe its working. It will supply, no doubt, a certain want. The workers must and will have amusements, and almost any systematic regulation of these matters is an improvement upon the casino and public house. Fears have been expressed lest access to the billiard table, chess board, draughts, &c., should foster a spirit of gambling, but as many can only enjoy themselves in such recreations, not having accustomed themselves to read and think, and as gambling and betting are strictly prohibited, it is surely better to amuse themselves under these conditions than at places where all the evils of gambling are allowed. Great care must be taken in appointing the managing body, for, doubtless, the success of the institution will depend wholly on its management. It is an interesting experiment, and may be looked on as one of the better movements of the year.[21]

Increasingly, however, as the period wore on, a more hard-line approach to the issue of working-class drinking and disreputable leisure behaviour generally emerges from the pages of Dare's *Reports*. This hardening of attitude can be traced in the following way. In 1859 he had asserted that moral means - the provision of rational recreations - were the best way of dealing with drinking. His attitude to repressive legislation was notably negative:

The taste of the working man for more rational amusements should be cultivated by every possible means; it is the only effectual way of modifying his excessive drinking habits. It is a doubt whether the partial closing of the beerhouses has not increased rather than diminished drinking. Stolen pleasures are sweet, and the idea that every glass thus obtained is in defiance of the authorities seems to give it an additional zest. Besides, when they can sit their own time, they do not toss it off at once like the prohibited draught. As the pretence for the beershops is that the working man may procure drink for domestic use, they should only be open on the Sabbath at dinner hour, and at none of them should ale at any time "be drunk on the premises." Beershops should also be at a certain fixed distance from each other, and their number should bear some proportion to the number of the inhabitants in their respective localities. But it must be confessed that little can be done by legislation to suppress drunkenness. Permissive bills and Maine liquor laws are mere quackery. It is simply not true that there is less drinking now than formerly in the State of Maine; and where a neighbourhood is fit for a Permissive Bill, it will no longer require it, as a majority of its inhabitants will have become abstainers before agreeing to adopt it; moral means are the only legitimate weapons for the reclamation of the drunkard.[22]

By 1866, however, though Dare still maintained that it was chiefly by counter-attractions that excessive drinking could be neutralized, it is clear that he had moved towards a more prohibitionist stance, regarding legislative measures - notably the Midnight Closing Act - in a more positive light:

The refusal to grant spirit licenses [sic] to a number of unnecessary beerhouses, and the stern caution given to others will produce good fruits. Instead of new licenses being granted, the old ones should be annulled wherever repeated infractions are discovered. While, generally speaking, I do not advocate coercive legislation, I do most strongly urge the enforcement of the "Midnight Closing Act." Late hours lead to all manner of vice and crime. The manslaughter in Wharf-street was committed after visits to various public houses till three or four o'clock in the

The 'Old Pack Horse' public house, Belgrave Gate, 1850s

morning, and the robbery of the night-mail directly after leaving a notorious concert hall. What can a quiet inland town like Leicester want of houses open all night long? How detrimental, both physically and morally, to the individuals, especially to working men, who haunt them. Those whose labours require them at six o'clock in the morning cannot have had sufficient repose to renovate their "thews and sinews," and fit them to resume their employment. Respectable householders do not require to be at public houses after twelve o'clock, either for relaxation or the transaction of business, nor do commercial travellers require them, as they have their accustomed hotels, to which at any hour they can gain access.

When attending the sick and dying I have frequently heard them complain of being disturbed by the brawls of drunkards at all hours, and disgusted to hear their loathsome language and filthy songs. Several respectable persons have told me that they have been obliged to remove their residence to escape such perpetual annoyance. Employers in a body, and, indeed, the inhabitants at large, should demand the enforcement of the Midnight Closing Act. This step would be a benefit to the publicans themslves, and as all houses would be closed there would be no jealousy as to custom amongst them. Parties who are only in the town during the hours of business can form no idea of its "night-side" doings. Let the Act be enforced, let immediate loss of license follow its infraction, it would soon wear a better aspect. The alteration of so many public houses into what are called "liquor vaults" is much to be deplored. Some of these places have been lately built, in defiance, apparently, both of magistrates and families who dwell in their neighbourhood. If a few of the proprietors were deprived of their licenses it would make the others more careful. And it would be a great blessing to the town if some check could be put upon the indiscriminate multiplication of the beershops. These places are many of them mere sinks of gambling, vice, and debauchery. As soon as a few houses are built, some of these drinking dens are opened and the new comers called "to be drunk on the premises." Here and there one sells only to out-door customers. As this was their original design, the whole of them should be restricted to it. As it is, they are stuck up in localities where the inhabitants whc use ale, &c., keep it in their own houses, and, therefore, as many respectable persons have said to me, they "do not want such places amongst them," but are perpetually annoyed by the drunkenness and disturbance which they create.[23]

By 1868, Dare was calling for increased legal action against publicans:

As regards the management of the licensed victuallers, it is with much satisfaction that I submit to our own able and respected magistracy the following very judicious remarks, delivered by the Hon. Captain Moreton, chairman, at the Hinckley Petty Sessions, September 7th. Before granting the licenses, the chairman at very considerable length addressed them, observing "that he could not congratulate them on the absence of crime. There had been in all ten convictions for using unjust measures. They might each consider themselves a centre of influence, either for good or evil, though he feared in the majority of cases it had been for the latter. His remarks had no reference to those who had been well conducted, but it had been proved that out of 172 convictions, from 82 to 85 had been the result of drunkenness." The chairman

Everard, Son and Welldon's Brewery, Southgate Street, 1870s

then proceeded to analyse the various crimes, remarking "that they presented a dark picture." He further enquired as to "who were the persons who chiefly depended on drunkards," intimating "that while some of the public houses were well kept, the majority were a disgrace. It formed the greater part of the work of the police to look out after public houses, and it was well known that the publicans kept scouts watching in the streets to give notice of their approach. There was also another side of the picture. There were the desolate houses and wretched wives, and the diseased children, all of which might be traced to drunkenness, and remotely to the publicans. It was also well-known that in only a few instances would a public house support a wife and family; the husband had to follow some other calling, leaving his wife and daughters at home to stand at the bar, and hear language the most disgraceful and abominable. It frequently happened that the husband falls a victim to the temptations that surrounded him, and the poor wife had either to drag her husband out of another public house, or out of the bowling alley attached to his own. For public houses to be kept as they should be, there should not be more than a quarter of the present number. It should be further remembered that the convictions did not represent a fourth of the crimes actually committed, and it became them so to exert their influence as to repress crime and reduce the county rate. Some of the publicans were in the habit of harbouring poachers, and others kept by them the instruments by which the poacher accomplished his work. In his (the chairman's) opinion, no woman ought to be allowed to keep a public house, and he wished there publicly to state that in future he would never sign a license where a woman only had the sole management. The convictions during the past year were then separately read over, the chairman intimating that the Bench had resolved that whenever a second conviction took place the license should be suspended." Mr. Crossland said he "concurred in every remark made by Captain Moreton." From long observation of these matters I am enabled to add my hearty approval. Let the publicans of every description know that loss of license shall inevitably follow the second conviction; there would soon be an improvement in conducting their traffic. It is to be hoped that the commendable plan of closing the market at 10 o'clock will lead to the enforcement of the Night-closing Act, or, at least for Saturday and Sunday nights.[24]

In 1869, alarmed by the increasing growth of drinking establishments in the town, Dare praised the work of the Brewster Sessions in dealing severely with disreputable licensees and supported Temperance calls for what amounted to an all out attack on the drink trade:

The following facts will show, perhaps, more fully than any general statement, our present social and religious manifestations. Reckoning the hospitals and certain school-rooms with the churches, there are sixteen places in which episcopalian service is celebrated; and the dissenters have forty-eight places of worship. What I wish to point out is, that while we have, in all, but sixty-four religious agencies, there are in the town five hundred and forty-five drinking establishments: they are as follows: -

Licensed Victuallers	*285*
Beer Houses	*243*
Wine Shops	*17*
	545

So that there are more than eight places for the sale of intoxicating liquors to one for divine worship. The drinking shops, too, are open all week as well as on the Sabbath day thus furnishing at all times opportunities for drink beyond all requirement; there being one of these places to about 180 of the inhabitants, reckoning men, women, and children. But as a great number of families, who live in the suburbs, and also a great number who live in the town, never frequent the drinking shops, the actual proportion is still more glaring. And hence the quantity of drink consumed by certain classes must be enormous. How is it possible for a few Missionaries to make any head against these ever increasing causes of ignorance, and drunkenness, and crime? It appears that the beer-houses and wine shops together, nearly equal in number the old regularly licensed establishments. They have all sprung up within a few years; nothing has arisen in our social condition to require such a number. They ought to be immediately reduced, one half at least, and the other half, if necessary at all, should only be allowed to sell to out-door customers. It should be made imperative, in any future alteration of the licensing system, that there shall be a fixed proportion between the inhabitants of a town and the number of public-houses; and also that they should be at certain distances from each other. And now that so many of the lower orders are admitted to the franchise, all drinking places should be closed during parliamentary and municipal elections. It is evident, from recent manifestations, that corruption is creeping into our boroughs. The drink-sellers are combining to send their own nominees into the council chamber. Many houses were open to "free and independent electors;" and nothing shows more fully the low mental and moral condition of voters, than the enquiry, "What good is the franchise to me, what shall I get by it?" We read of a Roman Emperor taxing curious commodities, but it was left for a Christian government, whose morality is guarded by a state paid church, to raise large portions of its revenues from the vices and degradation of its subjects; while it leaves them in the very ignorance that makes them the prey of those vices. I strongly endorse the following notice, by the Leicester Temperance Society, of the last Brewster Sessions: "An event, we had anxiously waited for, believing that the late Act of Parliament had given an effectual blow to publican audacity. Our anticipations have been realized, and the minds of all respectable householders relieved, by the fact, that all dealers in intoxicating liquors are brought under the surveillance of the magistrates. On this occasion, your Committee have exercised their influence in memorializing, and in other ways drawing the attention of the magistrates to those houses most noted for allowing drunkenness, gambling, and other immoral practices. We thankfully take this opportunity of recording our united thanks for the courteous manner in which they received the memorial, and the information tendered; and sincerely hope the warnings, threatenings, and withholding the licences from some of the worst houses, will have the desired effect. At the same time, we hope the corporation will encourage their public servants to do their duty in bringing delinquents to public justice. We think this is one step in the right direction, and are anxiously waiting for more stringent laws from the next parliament, when our Sabbaths will be freed from the unholy traffic." The promptitude of the magistrates produced a marked effect on the conduct of the beerhouse keepers. It is a pity that any of the suspended licences were renewed. Why should a strong fellow of indifferent character, with a good trade and plenty of work, throw it aside, and be allowed to set up one of these places, that he might lead an idle life and indulge his depraved tastes in dogs and gambling, in pugilists and drink? His house is within twelve steps of two others that are next door to each other, and directly opposite an old public house. Let it be borne in mind in all future applications for licences, that we have already more than eight drinking shops to one place of worship, and one to every 180 of the inhabitants, or in other words to every 45 families. The Bench, too, must still hold the rod "in terrorem," over the foul-mouthed ruffians who pollute our streets and public walks with obscenity. If a few respectable persons would make a point of seizing and prosecuting them, it would greatly tend to suppress the disgusting practice. They are silent at the approach of the police. Their own order will not impeach, and if neighbours who are known interfere, they take revenge by inflicting private injuries.[25]

By 1872 Dare was firmly of the belief that coercive legislation had led to a reduction in drunkenness and a quietening of the streets in the town. Calls for further legal restrictions against the drink trade, especially 'dram shops', were also made:

As I have frequently observed, it is a favourite, but not altogether sound, maxim that "people are not made wise and virtuous by legislation." Well, if it cannot help them in this direction, of what use is it? The fact is, legislation may do much by removing hindrances to improvement; by suppressing customs and institutions that foster vice; and by penalties against brutality, obscenity and drunkenness. The working of the new Licensing Act and others confirms these assertions. Since the enforcement of the former, I have made inquiries in different parts of the town as to its effect. "Oh! the street is not like the same," says one; "We are quiet enough now, especially on Saturday nights and Sunday mornings," says another; "I hope the Magistrates will strictly carry it out," utters a third. And I remember, on going from our discussion class on the first Saturday night it was enforced, I wondered why the North and Sanvey-gate were so still. Usually in that short distance there were two or three gatherings of men, women, and children, quarrelling, fighting, and uttering the most disgusting language. But on this night there was quiet, and has been ever since. Legislation has wrought the change. Applying to another busy locality, an intelligent and truly liberal-minded friend gives the following information:

"Residing in a much-frequented thoroughfare, near the centre of town, I am in a position to judge somewhat of the effects of the new Licensing Act, and have the pleasure of stating that, whereas before the new Act was put in force, the neighbourhood in which I live was almost always on Saturday nights, and during the early hours of Sunday mornings, greatly disturbed by the noise and quarrels of drunken brawlers, making night hideous with their cries, and so preventing my neighbours and myself from obtaining the rest needful after a long day's work. Since the new law has been put in operation, I have not heard one single midnight brawl, and at 12 o'clock on Saturday nights the neighbourhood has been as quiet as it formerly was on Sunday nights. There has also been a manifest decrease in the number of drunken persons passing along the streets."

These facts, I think, go far to justify what some people regard as repressive legislation, and prove that the new Licensing Act is a step in the right direction. If still further restriction could be placed over the dram shops, so much frequented by women and young girls, so as to check in some measure the dissipation practised by a large portion of our female population, a still greater good would result; for of all saddening sights, I think that of a woman in a state of intoxication is the most deplorable; and, personally, I should hail with pleasure any measure that should have the effect of leading, or even of compelling, our women to lead sober lives. As a further testimony in favour of the new law, I may say that a few days ago I was talking with the wife of a publican in my neighbourhood, and asked her how she liked the early closing? She said in reply that she was thankful for it, as she could now get a good night's rest, which before was almost impossible; but that she was not quite satisfied, as she would like to close all the day on Sunday. A similar judgement is almost universal in the town, for I have inquired as to the working of the Act wherever I have visited. A respectable householder, whose premises abut on a beershop, where the company consists chiefly of boys and girls under twenty, and which never ought to have been opened, exclaims, "Yes, we find the difference now; it is a shame that such mere youths should have been allowed to drink and dance all hours at such places; and the turning of so many public houses into 'spirit vaults' has been the ruin of many I could point out. The earlier closing is just right; our street is clear now before midnight." At a busy shop in a busy thoroughfare, a young lady informed me - "Since the new regulations we can close earlier, get to rest earlier, open earlier; and the whole neighbourhood is as pleasant again." In another street, a family on whom I have called for many years expressed deep satisfaction at the change: "The noise and drunkenness used to be awful, especially on Saturday night; men swearing and fighting, women screaming, 'We won't go home till morning,' and using the most outrageous expressions. We could get no sleep till three or four o'clock in the morning. We are so glad of the alteration; and if one-half of the beershops were closed, and the other half only allowed to sell out of doors, it would be better still."

Information obtained at the police stations confirms these statements. There have been fewer cases of drunkenness before the magistrates; the police can clear the streets with less trouble and danger than formerly, for as the last straw overpowers the camel, so the last glass infuriates the drunkard, causing annoyance to others, and often fatal resistance to the guardians of the public.

I have dwelt thus fully on this important social question, that the Magistrates might be strengthened in their determination to carry out the new Licensing Act in its entirety. It is to be earnestly hoped that they will not be led aside in the least, by the ex parte advocacy of hired professionals. Nor should they relax in punishing obscene language in our thoroughfares, for in these matters I fearlessly assert, that repressive legislation has produced the most beneficial influence.[26]

Finally, in 1873, Dare applauded the legal measures being taken against wine-shops and called for additional restrictions on other drinking places:

It is very satisfactory that the wine-shops, those dens of immorality, are being suppressed. Other drinking places should be in some proportion to the population, and none inscribed "to be drunk on the premises." Nor should public-houses be metamorphosed into gin palaces, or "spirit-vaults" as they are called, as they only encourage drinking; the original design of accommodation for business, rest, &c., being lost sight of entirely. It is to be hoped that legislation, both local and imperial, will be strengthened in these directions.[27]

Religion

Dare regarded religious sentiment as fundamental to working-class welfare and improvement. His *Reports* accordingly drew regular, albeit very brief, reference to the number of new or extended places of religious worship being established in the town. Most of his detailed comment on religious provision, however, is of a highly critical nature. He particularly attacked the many acts of 'unchristian bigotry' and 'spiritual tyranny' he witnessed, at the hands of insensitive, proselytizing, religious dogmatists. What emerges from these details, of course, is an important account of the sectarian rivalries which clearly prevailed in the town in the period, as evangelizing clerics went in search of working-class converts. In 1848, for instance, Dare noted:

In the religious world, the sectary is anxious to propagate certain opinions, and gain proselytes, rather than to awaken the religious sentiment that slumbers in every human heart. Or worse still, the Puseyite is darting about with his superstitious formalities, trying to lead captive the simple, and extend the spirit of popery.

In a house where I had been requested to call, I was informed that two clergymen had just made a visit. One of them urged a sick inmate, the father of the family, to confess to the other, as he would then "banish all his sins from him, like sinking them into a well." These words were used by the invalid's wife in giving me an account of the circumstances. The sick man refused to make confession, and very naturally inquired, "How it was that one of the reverend gentlemen couldn't give absolution as well as the other?" "Oh," replied the negative divine, "Mr.- is a Priest; he has received the power from Almighty God; I have not." The following fact illustrates "what manner of spirit" is at work for the extirpation of heresy, and the revival of the religious sentiment amongst the fallen masses of our poorer brethren. One day, a curate had just made a call where I usually visit. Some statements had been put forth by him which were controverted by the inmates of the house. "Oh," he answered, "I come to give instruction, if you are willing to receive it, not to enter into controversy. Argumentation with you would only degrade my office, and flatter your vanity." But we must expect such manifestations from individuals who estimate so meanly the ministerial office as to imagine that human power, whether sovereign or prelatic, can confer authority and dignity upon it. "Why do you attend Chapel?" asked one of these true successors of the Apostles of a poor woman: "you will not hear the Gospel there, you should come to Church to obtain the truth." She inquired how she could be assured of that. "Oh," he retorted, "the Bishop will see to that; he makes us preach the truth." "Well!" said another to a poor old person who has attended our Mission Chapel from its opening, and who is desirous of being a follower of the blessed Redeemer, "you may live seven years, but if you do, I will not read the burial service over you." I am sorry to be obliged to make these observations, but is this the best way of curing religious indifference? - of rooting out heathenism in the bosom of Christianity, and calling back the poor to "worship of their fathers"?[1]

For Dare, Christianity had to be presented in its 'primitive and practical simplicity' in order to be acceptable to the masses.[2] Proselytism failed in this respect, Dare maintained, and was counter-productive, since it tended to discourage, rather than encourage, religious sentiment amongst the working classes. He makes the point during the course of his detailed critique of Churchmen in 1849:

I am sorry that I am obliged to refer to certain acts connected with our evening service that are a disgrace to Christianity. But I wish it to be known that I shall expose and repel every slander and act of bigotry or spiritual tyranny I may meet with, from whatever quarter it may proceed. It will be remembered that at our last monthly meeting I informed you that a Rev. Gentleman had been to our door-keeper to say that he would not allow him to partake of the Sacrament any more at his Church, unless he desisted from attending as Sexton at the Mission Chapel. Accordingly the Rev. Gentleman called again on the Thursday before the sabbath when that beautiful rite was to be administered to repeat his injunctions. He added that he should also withhold the charity arising from the fund subscribed at this ordinance, in case the door keeper did not comply with his orders. All this was done in such an unkindly and authoritative manner that the poor man found it impossible to approach the Communion table again, though I had earnestly advised him to do so, if he found it to be his duty to attend. Accordingly he did not go, nor has he received the Sacrament there since this illegal, not to call it unchristian prohibition. The harsh and arbitrary conduct of the clerical functionary towards him has completely destroyed all spiritual interest associated in his mind with that venerable old temple of worship. Yet Churchmen wonder at Dissent, and thus vainly endeavour to suppress it. It appears, as I suspected, that a lady of respectable station had sent the rev. gentleman to issue his Christ-like commands and warnings - as that benevolent lady herself paid our door-keeper a visit about the same time to expostulate with him upon turning "Socinian," as she expressed it. She slanderously asserted that we deny Christ - that the institution in All Saints'

Mission rooms like this one on Dun's Lane - aimed at working-class religious redemption - became a familiar sight in Leicester in the period

Open was inimical to the Church; and that he would lose their charities if he continued his attendance at such a place. She wondered how a poor man, who was dependent for all he had, should dare to set himself up against his lawful minister. He replied that we did not deny the Saviour, for he had been himself to hear Mr. Berry, whose text at once showed the contrary. It was, "He that hath not the spirit of Christ is none of his:" and the sermon was in strict accordance with the sentiment of the passage. It was a beautiful discourse, and he did not believe the scandalous reports about his faith; nor would he give up his right to judge of spiritual concerns for any paltry temporal advantages they might offer or withhold. He knew, he said, that he was dependent upon man for what he enjoyed, but he knew at the same time that in a higher and better sense he was not, "for the earth was the Lord's and the fulness thereof." The agitation caused by these "fiery assaults" induced a relapse of a chronic disorder that disabled him for a long period from his daily labour, and it was only by the kind and skilful attention of a medical gentleman that he was restored to his family. I advise these, and others who, I understand, have been acting in a similar way as to my faith and principles, to leave me to the quiet discharge of my duties. I can assure them I have a deep sense of my responsibility. Obstructing none, I shall vindicate my own ministry from all interference.

The following is another sample: I had been requested to call on a poor young man, near death. I went; he had just breathed his last. After a little conversation with his aged mother, she told me that two curates had lately been to the house. She begged them to go up and see her dying boy; but they first began to inquire "whether any one had been to visit him?" The mother replied, "Only Mr. Butler, who had also attended his brother when he died a little time ago." She asked the curates three times in the course of their conversation to go up and see her son. They answered, "No! Mr. B.'s principles and theirs were very different, and they would not go up, unless she would order that man to keep away." This the poor woman could not, and would not do, as her family, with many others amongst the poor, had often experienced the kindness of that gentleman in seasons of affliction and death. She again entreated them "to see her boy," adding, "there is but one way to heaven, the path that Jesus marked and trod." "Ay!" the clerical functionary replied, "there is a way that seems right to man, but it leads to destruction;" implying that the only safe way was that pointed out by the inspired successors of the Apostles. The ordained divine then inquired if she had a "Common Prayer book"? She said "No, her family had been brought up dissenters." He promised to bring her a book. This he has forgotten to do. The two representatives of the "poor fishermen" then departed without having seen the sick man, who, according to their own unfeeling insinuations, was hastening to eternal damnation, and that because they had not been allowed to minister to his spiritual wants. This Christian exhibition occurred on a Friday. On the following Monday their spiritual superior, the Vicar, called himself. After asking how the sick man was, he made as if intending to go upstairs, but finding that the young man had just fallen into a deep sleep, he kindly desisted. The Vicar then proceeded to inquire who had attended him? And being informed, as above, he repeated nearly verbatim *the words of the two curates. He seemed to be filled with astonishment that such a man dare exercise the holy office and minister in things sacred, forgetting (it seems for the moment), that Paul was a tent-maker, that Peter caught fishes, and Christ was the "carpenter's son."*

By way of showing his own, and sole, right to such ministrations, he told the poor uninformed mother, who smiled at his self-complacency, that the Bishop had laid both his hands on his head and given him authority to preach the Gospel, and visit all the sick in the parish; she was therefore in duty bound to send for him, or his subordinates; he would come at any time, if she would first order Mr. Butler not to come again. This, as before, she said she could not do. The inspired possessor of the Holy Ghost continued, "He has no power! What does he do when he waits on the sick?" The mother replied, "He reads and prays by them." "But," again ejaculated the true descendant, "he has no power." The vicarious divine then departed. None of them had called again up to the time of my visit. The poor young man was then lying dead, unconscious of all this vain heartless mockery, that would be truly laughable, were it not in such close connection with the most solemn wants and feelings of our common humanity.[3]

So strong was Dare's antipathy towards proselytism, that he refused to allow a Maternal Society, run by one of the town's religious bodies, to use the Mission room:

A short time since, a deputation waited upon me from the Ladies' Committee of the "Maternal Society," connected with one of the religious bodies in this town, to know if they might use the mission room, to form a similar society in that locality. As I had for some time wished to have a "Mother's," or adult sewing branch, I thought that perhaps we might accomplish by co-operation what I felt convinced would be very serviceable to the mothers of families. But, on obtaining the rules of the "Maternal Society," I found that, though very commendable in itself, the ultimate object was to make proselytes, their meetings being wholly for religious purposes. They have since obtained another room for their praiseworthy efforts, but they seem hardly aware that there is a grade of mothers wholly beyond the pale of such influences, who should not be neglected, and who, indeed, can only be elevated to their standard by improving their domestic habits and social condition.[4]

Dare maintained that working men and women were resentful of clerical superintendence unless it was exercised in a 'generous and unsectarian way'.[5] Accordingly, he asserted that it was only by:

not meeting every honest expression of opinion, however erroneous, with overbearing dogmatism, or insolent denunciation, and showing sympathy for all the doubts and difficulties felt, and a calm and candid desire to weigh, and if possible remove them, that the neglected, and thinking can be led to feel an interest in the objects of the missionary.[6]

The refusal of certain religious functionaries to inter people, who had not been baptized, in consecrated ground, also incurred Dare's condemnation. The opening of the public

The Cemetery, Welford Road, opened 1849

Cemetery on Welford Road in 1849 was accordingly welcomed by him:

The Cemetery must not pass unnoticed. This beautiful place will be alike an ornament and protection to the town. It will afford the dead an undisturbed repose, and secure the living from the pestilential vapours of intramural sepulture. It will also increase our religious liberty by shielding us from the clerical insolence frequently manifested in relation to the ceremony of infant baptism.

Several cases of this nature have fallen under my notice. "Your child cannot be buried in consecrated ground unless it be baptized," said a clerical gentleman to a mother, whose infant was about seven days old. "But," she replied, "it has not been baptized, and it is dead, and has been buried." The ghostly man responded, "The Lord have mercy on its soul!" "There!" said another (after pouring a quantity of water on the head of a sickly child, which its grandmother was nursing), "your babe is now safe; if it should die, it will go to heaven." Another respectable parent, whom I know, was annoyed in the following manner: "Don't you know that if your child dies without being baptized, it will not go to heaven - it will be placed in a box, and put into a dark hole?" Recently, an infant was brought from its native village (a long way off) to this town to be buried, because, not having been christened, the minister of the place would not "pass it through the church." Two children were lately interred in a church-yard in this town. On coming to their graves, which were close together, to read the usual service, the minister inquired, "Whether they had been baptized?" Learning that the eldest had not, he turned his back upon its unconscious remains, and directed his services wholly to the other one - the mother of the neglected babe felt deeply wounded. I rejoice that the Cemetery has made a repetition of these insults impossible; and earnestly hope that some arrangement will be made to enable the poor of the lower parts of the town "to bury their dead" in its ample resting-place.[7]

Despite the efforts of the various religious functionaries in the town to gain converts, Dare drew attention in 1862 to the 'humiliating fact' that nearly one half of the population still attended no place of worship.[8] Yet Dare himself did not regard non-attendance at religious worship as an essential index of working-class irreligiosity. He argued in 1862, for instance, that:

It would be unjust to say that all who do not attend public worship have no religious convictions or sentiments. They have no antipathy to religion itself, but the popular belief no longer produces conviction.[9]

Remembrance card, 1866

Dare contended that:

The neglected classes possess a kind of traditional belief that has but little influence in shaping their actions, and is chiefly manifested in times of severe sickness, bereavement, or death.[10]

In addition, Dare regularly referred to the many expressions of natural religious sentiment and common humanity he witnessed amongst the working classes, even among the most depraved and vicious. In 1858, for instance:

Often, under a rough exterior, many sterling qualities are discovered, and the "milk of human kindness," though curdled by a mistaken sense of wrong, may, by Christian love, be made to flow in a healthful current. Nor must it be supposed that some of the best fruits of religion are not found amongst many who never attend any place of worship. I have known the watchers in a sick family, worn out with sorrow and want of sleep, allowed to go to rest, in a neighbour's bed, the inmates having left it the while, and come to watch over the dying. I have known a poor mother pale and attenuated through privation, with a child at her bosom, take the infant of another who was ill and more weakly than herself and give it suck. I have known a father, whose children had been driven from a Sunday school for want of better clothing, take his crust on the Sabbath and wander away into the forest to worship God in His own temple, under a sense of wrong inflicted by those who professed to be imbued with the spirit of Him who "despised not the poor"; yet neither privation nor sense of wrong could destroy his veneration for God or his love for the Saviour of the world.[11]

The point is re-affirmed in 1859, in an extract which is interesting for the way Dare describes the appeal of strange religious 'isms', such as 'Brownism', to the working classes:

As regards religion amongst the working classes, though, perhaps, there are but few who are wholly destitute of religious feeling, yet vast numbers attend no place of worship. The existing forms of belief and methods of religious teaching do not interest them. Others who have any religious sentiment are fond of "running after strange doctrines." One while it is "Mormonism," then "Spiritualism," or some other "ism," succeeds; and now, a favourite doctrine in the Midlands is "Brownism," recently started in Nottingham by an old pensioner named Brown, who is both lame and blind. Physical defects seem to be some of the requisites of the "Medium" and modern prophet. A shrewd working man, who is acquainted with the proceedings of this new religious body, informs me that this self-styled prophet professes to have received from Heaven instructions to form a "Circle of twelve members," who were convened for the first time at his house on the 19th July last year, which day, the whole members of the "Great Organisation," as they term themselves, are commanded by the angel Gabriel, to commemorate annually, as "That great day on which the foundation of the Universal church of Christ, and the new era in the morals of mankind was laid." It is the duty of the "circle" to propagate the revelations received from heaven and revealed on a scroll by Gabriel through the crystal to Brown. There are five towns or districts where they have members, Leicester reckoning the second. They profess to be governed entirely by "divine modern revelations." They hold services on Sunday, Monday, and Tuesday evenings, and the hymns, prayers, exhortations, and revelations they use, are all purported to be spiritually communicated to the prophet through the crystal by the angel Gabriel. The crystals, which are egg-shaped and of glass, are sold to enable members to procure revelations. Their leader publishes several periodical works which the members are expected to purchase at a rather high price. One of his serials is called the Scriptural Magazine, in which he professes to correct passages of Scripture.

As with Mormonism, the secret of success seems to be that the prophet promises his dupes a speedy possession of plenty and power. He teaches that all present laws are founded in tyranny and all religious sects in hypocrisy, that the Bible in its present form is a mass of corruption, and that the country will soon be overrun by a foreign enemy, when the spiritualists will be commissioned to destroy all the churches, chapels, bastilles and mansions of the great, and then take possession of the land and wealth for themselves. Their doctrines are a sad jumble of the vaticinations of Zadkiel and Dr. Cummings, mixed up with Owenism, Socialism, Swedenborgism, and divination of the crystal. There are already about one hundred Brownites in this town, who are very active in disseminating this wretched blasphemy. The best informed amongst them can scarcely read, and I have seen some letters written by the prophet's amanuensis, that make sad work with the simplest elements of syntax. Now all this is very lamentable, and no doubt originates in the neglect of early education and religious training.[12]

Yet, for many working-class people, religion evidently meant little at all and the sabbath was persistently 'desecrated'. In 1857, Dare presents a detailed argument on the theme, drawing attention to disreputable working-class activities which were a regular feature of Sunday town life. In the same account, Dare puts forward explanations as to why religious indifference occurred amongst the working classes:

Devoid of religious faith, a conceited and brutal scepticism prevails amongst large masses. Drunkenness and prostitution remain, I fear, undiminished. Cigar divans and British wine shops have much increased, and many of the public houses have recently opened large saloons, fitted up in attractive style, for the express purpose of alluring the young to the loose dance, or more abominable masquerade. The protracted dancing too, on the cricket-ground is a scene of utter demoralization. In the evening, especially in some parts of the town, respectable persons can scarcely pass without insult. On the Sabbath, the pigeon-flyer annoys the peaceful worshipper, the rat-hunter and dog-fancier are beating the river, or, secreted in some back room or remote field, are fighting their poor dogs, or "practising their young ones upon rats, whose teeth they have previously knocked out." The various outlets from the town are thronged with hundreds of the working classes, most of them with pipes in their mouths. Many of them are half-grown boys and girls, who, from early neglect and unrestrained feelings, exhibit the passions of mature age, and rush into connexions that entail poverty, sickness, and misery for life. Others of these Sunday strollers take the Reasoner, or Reynolds, with them, and are settling, with absolute decision, questions that the greatest minds never dare approach but with reverence and trusting faith; or, they are determining the destiny of the nation, while their own families are suffered to grow up in filth and rags. Others, generally those who neglect work at the proper time, are slily labouring on their allotments. I have observed also groups of drinkers, apparently married men, lurking around beer-houses during the time of divine service, for the purpose of giving notice of the

Interior of the Great Meeting Unitarian chapel on Bond Street in 1866

approach of the policeman, while their companions are drinking inside. They relieve one another at intervals, or some particular man is treated by the landlord to act as "touter" during the interdicted hours. I have seen the same parties, Sunday after Sunday, filling this post with a vigilance worthy of a better office. This custom is carried on in all parts of the town, and thus the authorities are baffled, and the Sabbath desecrated.

It will be remembered that a short time since, prizes were given for essays on the social condition of the poor, and the observation of Sunday in Leicester. The writers, for the most part, laboured to show the necessity and benefit of keeping the Sabbath as a day of rest and devotion, and the baneful effects of desecrating it. But none of them attempted to explain why working men, as a body, do not observe the Sabbath. Till the causes are known, it is not likely the effects will be removed. I have made several enquiries on the subject. An intelligent and religious man informs me that he has worked in, perhaps, forty shops. Whenever religion is mentioned in them, there is a general cry, "Oh! the parsons neither believe nor act as they preach; they make a trade of it; they are not the friends of poor men: they live in fine houses at a distance, and never come amongst us to chat with us, in a friendly way; if we are sick, they send their poor proud curates, who act and speak as if they were condescending, or they send the bigoted scripture reader, who pesters us with questions about our household affairs or private opinions, instead of sympathising with us, and imparting assistance."

Religion, with a few exceptions, is thus treated with ridicule, and everything of a spiritual nature is contemned with obscene language and scoffing blasphemy.

Now, these workshops, and other similar places, are the schools of some two or three thousand boys, who are set to work under, and for, these degraded men, as soon as they are seven or eight years of age. The little instruction they had gained at the day school, or may obtain in the Sunday school, is wholly countervailed by the harshness, ribaldry, and disgusting exhibitions of the workshop.

Winding boys are proverbially ill-used. As one boy can wind for four or five men, he has as many masters to please; frequently some are drinking or neglecting their work for days together. Then a rush is made to make up lost time, and as the boys cannot work when the men are idle, they are kept at times till the most unseasonable hours, and subjected to all kinds of brutal treatment. Driven early from home to work, he feels nothing of filial affection or parental control, and as his weekly earnings are added towards the support of the whole family, he soon thinks he can do better "on his own head;" so he breaks away from all restraint, and becomes his own master. He generally takes up his abode in some household where there are youths, of either sex, of similar age and habits. He has long left the Sunday School, he learns to scoff at religion, and the Sabbath is spent in the gratification of the lowest animalism.

There is a similar class of girls, in the seamers, and others who are sent from home while mere children, to nurse others as wretched as themselves. Errand boys, and those employed in brickyards, are of similar character. Thus a very numerous class are continually growing up; not only morally and spiritually neglected, but constantly under the most blighting influences. How is it likely, then, that they should become religious, or value the Sabbath? Another large class do not go to public worship because they have not the means to appear respectable. They think they are not welcome; the fustian shrinks from the "gold ring, and fine linen." Others, pressed by large families, cannot make the required payments, which are considerable amongst all voluntary bodies. A member of the church in one of our largest congregations, supplied me with the following list of annual payments in his sect:-

Four Quarterly Collections, morning and evening	8
School Sermons	2
Chapel Debt (sermons)	2
Tea Meetings	2
Gratuitous Trays, ditto	2
Home Missions	2
Foreign	2
Public Meeting, ditto	1
Academy (collections for)	2
Ordinance Collections	12
Benevolent Subscriptions	12
Foreign Missions (weekly)	52
Chapel Debt (weekly)	52
Sunday School Debt (weekly)	52
Pew Rents (quarterly)	4
Incidental (Town Mission, Poor, Chapels, &c.)	2
Annual Payments	209

The same thing applies to several societies that have lately been established for moral and *religious improvement. They all require money and a certain amount of intelligence to secure admission. Even amongst the sect who possess the least wealth, there are eighty annual payments.*

These facts are not referred to in a captious or unkindly spirit; they are commendable signs of zeal and determination to carrying out religious convictions. But they operate in keeping great numbers, who live from "hand to mouth," from attaching themselves to any religious body, and even from attending public worship. Other causes may be hastily enumerated, namely: excessive toil at some periods, and involuntary idleness at other times; the evil example of parents who care nothing about education or religion; too early release from parental authority; the habit of elder boys and girls sleeping from home through want of room; the ceaseless anxiety with numbers to procure their "daily bread;" the practical unbelief at the bottom of many institutions and practices in trade; the disgusting scenes tolerated in the Pasture, especially during the bathing season, the destructive habits of drinking and smoking, that are so fearfully increasing amongst the rising generation. These personal observations are corroborated by the remarks of an intelligent operative, who says in a note, "that his experience on the subject of religion as regards his own class, leads him to the following conclusions. One cause of neglect of worship is the lamentable prevalence of infidelity, which prevails to an extent few can conceive, who have not mixed with all classes on common ground; the leaven has been infused, and may be seen making its pernicious progress; it may be traced particularly amongst the working classes, in its various stages, from flippant criticism to unqualified atheism. Another cause is the effect of habit; nothing is more the effect of habit than attending a place of worship, and where this habit has been implanted in early life, many, though not religiously disposed, continue to observe it. "For my own part," he adds, "there was a time when I could not have spent the Sunday without attending a place of worship three times. Now, change of place has brought change of habit, and although my predilections in favour of religion are as strong as ever, yet the habit of non-attendance seems confirmed. There is a class of persons who object to attend because of the inconsistent conduct of those who do attend, but where there is a disposition to attend, such considerations would have no weight; that, I believe to be the great secret, - want of disposition. There is no cause more conspicuous than the want of disposition and the love of pleasure or excitement. Idle indulgence in parents, I think, is the cause of these causes. So long as they instil by example and precept, a reverential attachment to the place of worship, and regard for the Sabbath, there is little danger from atheism, but neglect of religious teaching renders the young an easy prey. There may be some who absent themselves for want of proper clothing, but that class are few in number. It must be confessed, however, that the general mind is not in harmony with religious worship, and I have little hope for the adult generation. The remedy seems to lie chiefly with the parent and Sunday School teacher. It is in the Sunday School, and at the domestic hearth where the reform must be carried out."

These are some of the principal causes of irreligion and Sabbath desecration; or, as Foster terms it, of "heathenism in the bosom of christianity." But, undoubtedly, the chief is neglect of the young. Till these causes are removed, society will continue to present the same revolting anomalies already described. The rising generation must be instructed, and all instruction must be combined with religious teaching, with the religion of the blessed Redeemer of the world. I have but little sympathy with the Sunday League. Not that I think they wish to secularize the day of rest, or assimilate it to the continental Sabbath. But it is beginning at the wrong end: they are trying to produce, by external means, what can only be effected by internal, and religious influences. What care the neglected and brutalized about grand music, or fine pictures, or relics of antiquity, or even the wonders of nature? They gaze with brutal indifference upon the beautiful earth, and more magnificent heavens. It is the inward that fashions the outward, the cultivated and devout spirit that "feels after God" in these things, and finds even in the tiniest flower a subject of delight and adoration.[13]

Finally, the poor condition of Sunday Schools was evidently a noticeable feature of the period, as Dare reported in 1872:

Sunday schools are not in a sound condition. Complaints of desertion are universal. This is a very discouraging fact, and arises chiefly, I think, from this cause - the scholars, generally speaking, do not belong to the parents of the respective congregations. Numbers are, too much, made the test of success. Were Sunday School children the offspring of the members of the congregations who conduct them, instead of being drawn from children whose parents are unconnected with them, and who ramble about at will, there would not be so many desertions after the school age. As soon as children of straitened means get a smart "set-out," they are off to distant and finer associations; but altered circumstances soon cause them to fall away. Very few secure lasting connections. Let Sunday-Schools proper belong to congregations, and let the dwellers in courts and frequenters of hedges and highways be collected on the Sabbath by missionaries, in their respective localities. This plan would lessen desertion, and as Board Schools with secular instruction will be demanded, all children must be sent to Sunday Schools for direct religious teaching.[14]

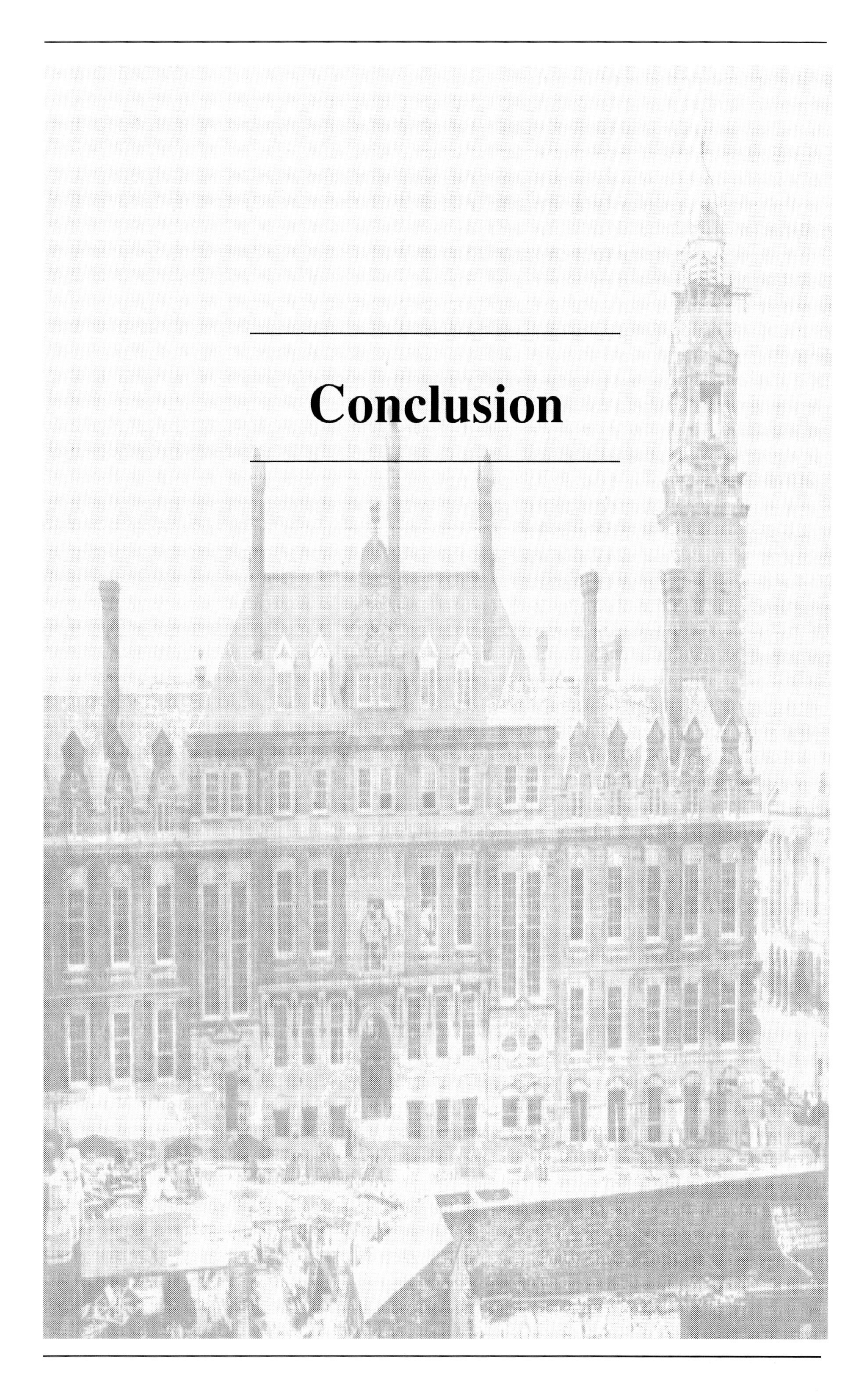

Conclusion

The Old Haymarket from Humberstone Gate, 1861

Conclusion

The period 1845-77 was clearly one of dramatic change in Leicester's history. The population doubled to over 100,000,[1] and the town's industrial base also expanded, especially with the rapid development of the footwear and allied elastic-web industries. Yet, at the same time, few factories were established and the bulk of the workforce continued to be employed in domestic or workshop production methods.[2] Consistent with the trend elsewhere in English society during this period, Leicester witnessed an increasing momentum towards the creation of a more 'respectable' society.[3] At the centre of this drive was the desire to make the working classes conform to a pattern of life based on middle-class values of self-help, diligence, industry, sobriety, education, rational recreation and religion. Many local voluntary and official bodies, directed towards achieving this goal, were established in Leicester in the period. The Leicester Domestic Mission, under the auspices of the dedicated missionary, Joseph Dare, was at the forefront of the movement.

From the 1860s onwards Dare detected that many members of the working classes were increasingly taking advantage of the facilities for improvement in the town and becoming more 'respectable': educating themselves and their children; attending religious worship; enjoying rational recreations; saving for a 'rainy day'; leading self-reliant, industrious lives, with happy families and cared-for children, in tidy, healthy homes.

In contrast, of course, there were many - the 'rough'- who remained outside the pale of improving influences. They lived in hovels, were uneducated and led reprobate, drunken lives, pursuing all manner of vice and criminal activity. They were idle and improvident, regularly worshipping at the altar of St.Monday and preying upon charitable individuals and institutions. Desertion, common-law marriage, wife-beating, illegitimacy and infant mortality were rife amongst this class. Wives and mothers had no knowledge of domestic management, health and hygiene, and increasingly drank spirits in 'free and easy's'. Their children were particularly vulnerable. Whilst babies, they were often 'cared for' by disreputable, drunken nurses and doped on cocktails of 'Godfrey's cordial' or laudanum. Infrequently attending school and removed ultimately whilst very young, they were forced to work long, arduous hours in disreputable work-places for poor wages, at the hands of cruel, exacting masters. Such children had 'no joyous sunny period' of youth. They were socialised into drinking, vice and crime very early on. Undisciplined, ill-fed, neglected and ill-treated, they left home when only adolescent, made improvident, early marriages, lived in hovels, and in turn, reared children in the same neglectful manner as they had been. Thus, the rough formed a 'race', doomed to 'hereditary' poverty, vice, crime, disease and early death. Shoe operatives generally, the lower ranks of hosiery workers, such as winders and seamers, errand boys, brickyard workers, box-makers and trimmers formed a major part of this class. Worst of all, however, were the 'dangerous and neglected denizens of lodging-houses and dwellers in overshadowed and overcrowded places not fit for human habitation'.[4] Into this category, Dare placed the permanent mendicants, many of whom were Irish.

Yet Dare himself acknowledged the fallibility of this stereotypical, moral dichotomy of the working classes, recognising that the general insecurity of working-class life in the period made the dividing line between the rough and the respectable a very fine, indeed arbitrary one. Referring to the many commercial depressions and the chronic under-employment in the staple hosiery trade which affected Leicester throughout the period, Dare recognised how poverty could

Belgrave Gate from the top of the Clock Tower, 1868

View of Leicester looking East over Silver Street, taken from the top of St. Martin's Cathedral c.1860

very easily force the respectable into the ranks of the so-called rough: how the respectable worker who found himself on short time for a sustained period would have to move district and cram into small, overcrowded, unhealthy dwellings in order to save on rent; how savings would soon disappear on daily needs; how clothing and furniture would have to be pledged; how numbers would be forced ultimately into the workhouse or driven to begging; how idleness, though involuntary to begin with, would soon become confirmed by repetition; how indifference as to their moral condition generally would set in, such that even in seasons of prosperity, many never recovered their better habits.

Living conditions, for many, remained appalling throughout the period and Dare recognised that the growth of disreputable places of amusement in the town were real temptations, intoxicating especially those raw, vulnerable, disorientated immigrants to the town, who accounted for the bulk of Leicester's population growth in the period.[5]

Dare's humanitarian concerns made him well aware that it was far too easy to condemn the working classes for their moral failings. The trick was to find good even in the apparently darkest of hearts. And this Dare surely did. His persistent references to the common humanity to be found even amongst the most neglected and depraved make this clear. Yet, at the same time, of course, it seems clear that Dare's attitude towards those who seemed to be making no headway towards improvement did harden. His increasingly repressive approach to drink perhaps indicates this, though, again, it has to be said that this was aimed as much at the providers of drink as at the drinkers themselves - arguably more so.

Dare's complex social philosophy, therefore, in many respects, represents a radical reappraisal of many of the views held by his contemporaries. He refused to proselytize and he regularly condemned the unchristian attitudes and acts of bigoted, evangelizing clerics. Whilst he joined his contemporaries in regarding respectability as a moral yardstick with which to judge working-class life, the shortcomings of popular culture being defined in terms of drunkenness, irreligion and improvidence, he did not fully accept that the physical facts of poverty, bad housing and disease could be viewed simply as effects, whose root causes were totally to be found in cultural depravity. For Dare, such a view was clearly far too simplistic. Maintaining that moral manifestations arise from circumstances, he could accordingly view drinking, ignorance, irreligion and moral depravity generally, not as causes, but rather as the legitimate consequences of, and the natural responses to, physical and economic privation. It was a position Dare never lost sight of. As late as 1873, he was still maintaining that the physical atmosphere had to be 'purified', before the 'moral atmosphere can be much improved.' Dare recognised that external physical and economic forces, beyond the control of the working classes, clearly played a central part in the determination of working-class respectability as much as moral factors. He acknowledged that respectability as a moral code offered little natural defence against the fundamental economic and physical insecurities of working-class life. It has been argued that respectability provided the ruling classes in the period with a means of escaping moral responsibility for the shortcomings of a free-market, capitalist, economy.[6] Dare's radical thinking, however, all too often urged employers and governments - both central and local - to face up to their responsibilities.

References

The Market Place and Corn Exchange, 1870s

Introduction

1. This short biography is based on Mrs I.C.Ellis' account of her grandfather in her *Records of Nineteenth Century Leicester*, (Leicester, 1935), chapter two.
2. It was raised to £100 in 1865.
3. They lived here till 1874, when they moved to Soar Lane Cottage, thence to 23 West Street in 1875.
4. *Leicester Chronicle*, 14.11.1840. *Appendix 1* lists the officials of the Mission, among whom representatives of Leicester's elite will be noted - the hosiers, Biggs, Walker and Kempson, the worsted spinners, Brewin, Whetstone and Fielding Johnson, the engineer, Gimson, the Town Clerk, Samuel Stone, the banker, Paget, for instance. The Unitarian influence was still evident in the 1870s - see: John Storey, *Historical Sketch of Some of the Principal Works and Undertakings of the Council of the Borough of Leicester, 1836-95*, (Leicester, 1895).
5. Tuckerman's ideas are expressed in his: *The Principles and Results of the Ministry at Large in Boston*, (Boston, Mass., USA, 1838); and *Joseph Tuckerman on the Elevation of the Poor: a Selection from his Reports* (Boston, Mass., 1874). See also: Ian Sellers, 'Unitarians and Social Change', in *The Hibbert Journal*, vol.61, 1962-3, pp.124-5.
6. Cited in J.Simmons, 'A Victorian Social Worker: Joseph Dare and the Leicester Domestic Mission', in *Transactions of the Leicestershire Archaeological and Historical Society*, XLVII, 1970-1, p.66. Simmons also notes that the history of the Manchester mission has been written by H.E.Perry: *A Century of Liberal Religion and Philanthropy in Manchester*, (Manchester, 1933), and that a large number of the Mission's reports are held in Manchester Central Library. The Liverpool Society's *Reports* for 1837-75 and 1900-37 are in Liverpool Record Office - Acc.2072. The history of the Birmingham Mission is given in H.New, *Hurst Street Domestic Mission, Birmingham*, (Birmingham, 1890). Birmingham Reference Library has a number of the Mission's reports for the period 1840-1938. A copy of the first report of the Leeds Mission (1845) is in the British Museum Library and Leeds Reference Library has one of the 11th, 1855. Records for the London and Bristol Missions appear to be non-existent; Simmons, *ibid.*, p.79.
7. J.A.Banks discusses the notion in 'The Contagion of Numbers', in H.J.Dyos and M.Wolff (eds.), *The Victorian City*, (R.K.P., 1976), volume 1, pp.105-22.
8. *Census Returns*, 1801, 1841.
9. So severe had the distress become by 1844, that local framework knitters had successfully petitioned the government for a public inquiry into their condition. See the *Report of the Commissioner appointed to Inquire into the Condition of the Framework Knitters, Parliamentary Papers*, XV, 1845.
10. Most notable of local Chartist leaders was Thomas Cooper. Details of Chartist activity in Leicester are given in his autobiography: *The Life of Thomas Cooper* (London, 1882).
11. Most *Reports* begin with a list of the Mission's officials for the year, followed by a short 'Committee Report', then Dare's report. They conclude with a list of subscribers and donations. The final *Report*, for 1877, was written by H.T.Basford, Dare's replacement as missionary. Two sets of the *Reports* survive: one is in Leicester Reference Library, Bishop Street - the *Reports* for 1869-70 (the 25th) and 1870-1 (the 26th) are missing from this collection; the other set is in the Great Meeting Library, Bond Street.
12. Dare was not a systematic writer and the *Reports* often meander through themes and details with a certain amount of overlap. The presentation of a series of representative, edited extracts from the *Reports* enables their repetitious nature to be avoided. Dare's syntax, spelling and punctuation have been retained.

Section I: The Work of the Leicester Domestic Mission

NB: the year refers to the *Report*

1. 1852, p.4.
2. 1857, p.12.
3. 1849, p.8.
4. 1857, p.3.
5. 1848, p.24.
6. 1846, p.6.
7. *Ibid.*, pp.17-23.
8. 1851, pp.15-16.
9. 1862, pp.12-13.
10. 1846, pp.20-1.
11. *Ibid.*, p.18.
12. 1854, p.13.
13. 1849, pp.10-11.
14. 1846, p.20.
15. 1850, pp.8-9.
16. 1859, pp.14-15.
17. 1875, pp.5-6.
18. 1850, pp.12-13.
19. 1874, p.18.
20. 1857, p.3.
21. 1867, p.14.

22. 1868, pp.18-19.
23. 1854, p.5.
24. 1876, p.6.
25. 1865, pp.19-20.
26. 1853, p.5.
27. 1865, p.29.
28. 1846, p.14.
29. 1854, p.11.
30. 1874, p.22.
31. 1876, p.6.
32. *Ibid.*, p.10.
33. 1846, p.3.
34. 1847, p.18.
35. 1857, p.3.
36. The figure is based on Dare's own estimates, as given, for instance, in 1854.
37. 1856, p.15.
38. 1854, pp.6-20.
39. 1847, p.13.
40. 1864, p.23.
41. 1872, p.3.
42. 1860, pp.3-4.
43. 1855, p.9.
44. 1847, pp.19-20.
45. 1855, p.9.
46. 1867, p.17.
47. *Ibid.*
48. 1868, pp.17-18.
49. 1877, p.5.
50. *Ibid.*, pp.12-13.
51. *Ibid.*, p.10.

Section II: Working-Class Life

Introduction

1. 1846, pp.5, 24.
2. 1852, p.6.
3. 1860, p.9.
4. 1854, p.16.

Employment, Poverty and Charity

1. 1852, p.6.
2. 1858, pp.5-12.
3. 1868, p.14. Dare's view that chronic under-employment was a persistent feature of the hosiery industry in Leicester in the period is borne out by the conclusions of the *Report of the Commission appointed to Inquire into the Truck System*, in 1871. See *Parliamentary Papers*, XXXVI, 1871.
4. 1859, p.5.
5. 1853, pp.7-8.
6. 1846, p.14, for instance.
7. 1856, p.6.
8. *Ibid.*
9. 1861, p.5.
10. 1859, p.20. Few factories in fact existed in Leicester prior to the 1880s. Both the hosiery and footwear trades were, on the whole, organised on domestic or workshop production lines. The elastic web industry, however, was mainly factory-based. Interestingly, industrial relations in this trade were poor. See: J.B.Haynes, 'A Study of Social Perceptions and Attitudes in the Context of Class Relationships in Mid-Victorian Leicester', (M.Phil. thesis, Leicester University, 1988).
11. 1862, p.3.
12. 1861, p.5.
13. 1862, pp.6-8.
14. They did not always materialize, however, as in 1854 and 1858.
15. 1866, p.3.
16. 1855, pp.6-7.
17. 1854, pp.10-11.
18. 1865, p.23.
19. 1855, pp.9-13.
20. 1864, pp.11-12.
21. 1866, pp.7-8.
22. 1848, p.10.
23. 1872, pp.7-10. Dare had for many years called for the setting up of a 'Mendicity Society' in Leicester, to organise and distribute local charity more systematically. He clearly supported the aims of the Charity Organisation Society, and welcomed the setting up of a local branch in the town in 1876. Dare was on the original committee of the body.

Environment and Health

1 1846, pp.23-4.
2. 1847, p.20.
3. 1848, pp.8, 21-2.
4. 1852, pp.8-11. The worst localities were evidently in Belgrave Gate, and inhabited chiefly by lodging-house residents and the Irish. The 'Wise Woman of Wing', in Rutland, was Amelia Woodcock. She was reputed to have committed suicide in 1867 on account of the persistent accusations of witchcraft against her. See: R.Palmer, *The Folklore of Leicestershire and Rutland*, (Sycamore Press, 1985), p.75.
5. 1865, pp.21-2. Writing in 1868, Dare found it 'inconceivable' that houses were still being built with 'no plan of self-acting ventilation' and with 'immovable top-sashes' -1868, p.11.
6. 1862, pp.9-10.
7. 1869, p.11.
8. 1874, pp.13-14.
9. 1864, pp.14-16.
10. 1869, pp.14-15. The Leicester Anti-Vaccination League was formed in 1869. For the history of the movement and details of the alternative 'Leicester method' for dealing with smallpox, see: J.T.Biggs, *Leicester: Sanitation versus Vaccination*, (London, 1912).
11. 1866, pp.14-15.
12. 1873, pp.13-14. The issue of child

mortality, as well as a 'glowing' account of the work of the local Board of Health, are dealt with in detail by M.Elliott, *Victorian Leicester*, (Phillimore, 1979).

13. 1875, pp.9-11.
14. 1876, pp.11-13.
15. 1868, pp.8-9. Presumably the Dispensary, to which Dare was referring, was that listed in the *Leicester Directory*, 1870, on East Bond Street.
16. 1867, pp.16-17. The headquarters of the Nurses Institution is given in the 1870 *Leicester Directory* as 84, Rutland Street.
17. 1866, pp.9-11.
18. 1862, p.4.
19. 1866, p.4.
20. *Ibid.*
21. 1873, p.14, for instance. Dare often gave the numbers of new houses being built.
22. 1866, p.4.
23. 1874, p.10.
24. 1872, pp.10-12. The newly built-up areas, to which Dare was referring, were part of the Dannett's Hall Estate developed by the Leicester Freehold Land Society. For more details, see Elliott, *op.cit.*, pp.115-6.
25. 1873, pp.14-16. The 'unsightly buildings', to which Dare was referring, were those of the Fever and Smallpox Hospital, erected in 1871 on Groby Road.
26. 1876, pp.8-9. The Flood Prevention Works were put into operation by the Corporation in 1873. See: J.Storey, *op.cit.*, pp.75-92.

Education

1. 1851, pp.7-8. Dare undertook a similar survey as part of his enumerator duties in the 1861 Census. His conclusions then revealed that more than half of working-class children were not being educated on a regular basis. See: 1861, p.15.
2. 1854, p.16.
3. 1848, p.6. The Mechanics' Institute in Leicester never had a strong working-class following. It was closed in 1870. See: J.Simmons, *Leicester Past and Present*, volume 2, (Eyre Methuen, 1974), pp. 31-2.
4. 1869, pp.6-7. The School of Art and Design was originally on Pocklington's Walk. The Working Men's College was the work of the Reverend David Vaughan, Anglican minister of St. Martin's. It was originally sited in Union Street. For its history, see: A.J.Allaway, *Vaughan College, Leicester 1862-1962*, (Leicester University Press, 1962).
5. 1867, pp.5-8. The debate was part of the build up to the Education Act of 1870. For more details on how the political issues were greeted in Leicester, see: G.T.Rimmington, *Education, Politics and Society in Leicester, 1833-1903*, (Nova Scotia, 1978).
6. 1868, pp.5-6. This Act was particularly important since most of Leicester's workforce was employed in domestic or workshop production; both the hosiery and footwear trades were organised in this way. See: Haynes, *op.cit.*
7. 1875, pp.6-7. The first seven Board Schools were on: Syston Street, King Richard's Road, Oxford Street, Slater Street, Elbow Lane - all 1874; Belgrave Road and Archdeacon Lane - both 1875.
8. 1876, p.7. The school, the Wyggeston Boys' Grammar School, was on Highcross Street, in the building occupied by the present Leicester Grammar School. The school was opened in 1877. The Wigston's Girls' School was opened a year later. In 1874, E.S.Ellis, speaking on behalf of the Wyggeston Charity, had stated that the proposed secondary school would 'advocate the speedy erection of Huxley's ladder from the gutter.' (*Leicester Journal*, 20.3.1874). Thomas Huxley, to whom he was referring, believed in the intellectual potential of the working classes, regarding them as a 'vast reservoir of untapped ability'. He accordingly advocated the establishment of a 'great educational ladder, the bottom of which shall be the gutter, and the top of which shall be the University' (*School Board Chronicle*, I, 1870, p.7).

Recreation

1. 1850, pp.19-20.
2. 1849, p.13. The Temperance Hall was erected on Granby Street in 1853. A leading light in the local Temperance movement was Thomas Cook, the pioneer of domestic and foreign travel.
3. 1848, pp.5-6.
4. 1864, p.7.
5. 1868, pp.12-13. The Half-Day Holiday movement had been active in Leicester since the 1850s. For details of it, see: Haynes, *op.cit.*
6. 1846, p.25.
7. 1859, p.6.
8. 1864, pp.8-9.
9. 1866, pp.3-4.
10. 1868, pp.4-5.
11. 1876, p.7.
12. 1874, pp.6-7. The working classes traditionally bathed in the river or canal at Abbey Meadows and St. Margaret's Pasture.
13. 1864, pp.6-7. The Museum on New Walk was originally opened in 1849.

14. 1850, pp.13-16.
15. 1873, pp.11-13. The Free Library was opened in 1870, on Belvoir Street, in the building previously used by the Mechanics' Institute - this was terminated. It is now the Central Lending Library.
16. 1876, p.7.
17. 1864, p.8.
18. 1867, pp.9-11.
19. 1865, pp.9-14. Two of the earliest known singing saloons in Leicester, and probably those to which the description refers, were the 'Alhambra Music Hall', on Belgrave Gate, owned by a Dan Cooke, and the 'Old Cheese Concert Hall', also on Belgrave Gate, owned by a William Paul. For more details on these see: H. and R.Leacroft, *The Theatre in Leicestershire,* (Leicestershire Libraries, 1986).
20. 1867, p.8.
21. 1866, pp.6-7. The location of this Club remains a mystery!
22. 1859, pp.6-7.
23. 1866, pp.4-5.
24. 1868, pp.7-8.
25. 1869, pp.8-10.
26. 1872, pp.5-7.
27. 1873, p.10.

Religion

1. 1848, pp.8-10. Leicester had a notable 'Puseyite' at this time in the Reverend W.H.Anderdon, vicar of St. Margaret's. For details of his career see: Anon, *A Brief Memoir of Father W.H.Anderdon*, (Leicester, 1890).
2. 1849, p.5.
3. *Ibid.*, pp.15-18.
4. 1856, p.11.
5. 1849, p.8.
6. 1858, p.17.
7. 1849, p.7.
8. 1862, p.3.
9. *Ibid.*, p.5.
10. 1851, p.4.
11. 1858, pp.17-18.
12. 1859, pp.15-17.
13. 1857, pp.6-11. The Sunday League originated in Leicester in the mid-1850s. It sought to provide rational recreations on the sabbath as a means of counteracting disreputable Sunday amusements. It was pioneered by Sir Joshua Walmsley, one of Leicester's M.P.'s at the time. He promoted a Sunday Recreations Bill in parliament in 1856. For more details see: Haynes, *op.cit.* and the *Leicester Chronicle*, 23.2.1856.
14. 1872, pp.15-16. Cf. also 1852, pp.19-20.

Conclusion

1. In 1851 Leicester's population was 60,642. By 1871 it was 95,220 and by 1881 it was 122,376. *Census Returns*, 1851, 1871, 1881.
2. Leicester's proto-industrial situation represents an interesting example of that 'broad handicraft basis' which Samuel has considered crucial for the English Industrial Revolution. See: R.Samuel, 'Workshop of the World: Steam Power and Hand Technology in Mid-Victorian Britain', *History Workshop*, 3, 1977.
3. See, for instance: T.R.Tholfsen, *Working-Class Radicalism in Mid-Victorian England*, (London, 1976); C.O.Reid, 'Middle-Class Values and Working-Class Culture in Nineteenth-Century Sheffield', (unpublished Ph.D thesis, Sheffield University, 1976); F.M.L.Thompson, *The Rise of Respectable Society*, (Fontana, 1988).
4. 1873, p.6.
5. See: J.Simmons, *op.cit.* (1974), p.6.
6. See: C.O.Reid, *op.cit.*, pp.65-82.

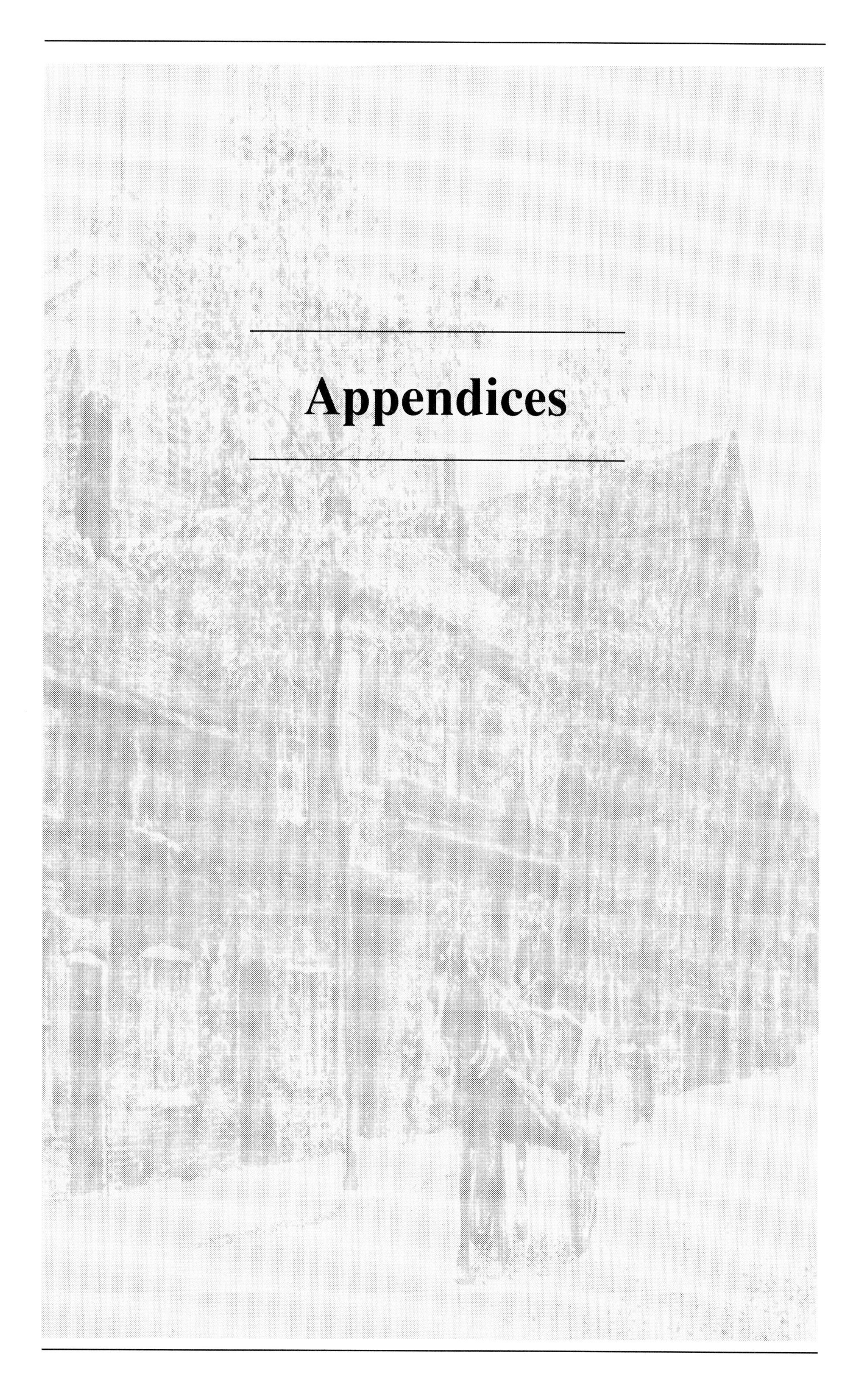

Appendices

Bridge Street towards West Bridge c.1880

Appendix 1

Officials of the Leicester Domestic Mission

Presidents

Joseph Whetstone (1846-7)
Thomas Paget (1847-52)
Reverend Charles Berry (1852-9)
C.Smith (1859-60)
Reverend C.C.Coe (1860-66)
T.F.Johnson (1866-9)
E.Clephan (1869-72)
H.Lees (1872-4)
W.Kempson (1874-5)
Reverend R.L.Collier (1875-6)
Reverend J.P.Hopps (1876-7)

Secretaries

W.H.Walker (1846-56)
E.Gittins (1846-66)
W.Kempson (1866-69)
A.Else (1869-72)
E.B.Gittins (1872-7)

Treasurers

J.Whetstone (1854-6)
E.Clephan (1856-77)

Domestic Missionaries

Joseph Dare (1845-76)
Henry T.Basford (1876-7)

Committee Members

Reverend C.Berry (1846-77)
S.Stone (1846-74)
W.Biggs (1846-67)
T.Paget (1846-75)
Mr Daniell (1846-8, 1851-2)
Joshua Biggs (1846-51)
W.Kempson (1846-77)
E.Clephan (1846-77)
J.Whetstone (1846-68)
E.Gittins (1846-77)
W.H.Walker (1846-56, 1867-77)
J.F.Hollings (1847-62)
R.Marshall (1847-63)
J.Flower (1851-62)
Mr Else (1851-4)
T.F.Johnson (1852-77)
F.T.Mott (1852-77)
C.Smith (1852-77)
Mr Spurrett (1852-4)
Mr Elgood (1852-3)
Mr How (1853-5)
A.Paget (1854-77)
R.Brewin (1854-76)
W.Whetstone (1854-77)
Mr Pollard (1854-5)
Reverend C.C.Coe (1855-77)
H.Riley (1862-77)
J.Matts (1862-77)
Reverend W.Mitchell (1867-9)
T.Coltman (1867-77)
T.Garner (1867-77)
E.F.Cooper (1869-77)
A.Else (1872-77)
G.Atkins (1872-77)
T.Raworth (1874-7)
J.Gimson jnr. (1876-7)
A.H.Paget (1876-7)

Appendix 2

Subscribers to the Leicester Domestic Mission

At the end of each *Report* a list of annual subscribers to the Mission - with their respective amounts - is given. The confines of space prohibit giving a complete list of all those who subscribed over the period 1845-77. The following extract illustrates the information given each year. It is taken from an 'average income' year - 1873-4.

	£	s	d		£	s	d
Atkins, Mr		10	6	Pollard, Mr John	1	0	0
Bankart, Miss		5	0	Paget, Mr T.T.	10	0	0
Brewin, Miss	1	0	0	Paget, Mr Thomas	5	0	0
Burberry, Miss		10	0	Paget, Mr A.	2	0	0
Bolus, Mrs		5	0	Paget, Mrs H.	2	0	0
Coltman, Mr T.		5	0	Parker, Mr J.	1	0	0
Coltman, Mr T.jun.	1	1	0	Paget, Miss C.	2	0	0
Clephan, Mr E.	2	0	0	Paget, Miss E.S.		10	0
Cooper, Mr E.F.		10	0	Rowlett, Mr		10	0
Cumberland, Mr	1	0	0	Rowlett, Mr W.T.	1	1	0
Carryer, Mr Joseph	1	1	0	Russell, Mr B.		10	0
Else, Mrs	1	0	0	Ride, Mr S.		10	0
Else, Mr A.		10	0	Raworth, Mr T.		10	0
Forrest, Mr T.B.	1	1	0	Stone, Mr S.	5	0	0
Fielding, Mrs J.	1	1	0	Spurrett, Mrs	2	0	0
Forrest, Mr S.	2	0	0	Simpson, Miss	2	0	0
Glover, Mrs		10	0	Stone, Misses	3	0	0
Gimson, Mr Josiah	1	1	0	Scott, Mr		5	0
Graham, Mr	1	0	0	Smith, Miss A.		10	0
Gilson, Mrs H.	3	0	0	Smith, Mr C.		10	0
Gimson, Miss		5	0	Stimson, Mr W.	1	1	0
Gittins, Mr E.B.		10	6	Stone, Miss K.		10	0
Hottinger, Miss	1	0	0	Scott, Mr Thomas		10	0
Hodges, Mrs	1	0	0	Smith, Mr J.A.		10	6
Johnson, Mr H.	1	0	0	Tarratt, Mr H.		10	0
Ison, Mr		2	6	Whetstone, Mrs	1	0	0
Johnson, Mr T.F.	5	5	0	Whetstone, Mr	5	0	0
Kirby, Mr F.J.F.		10	6	Warburton, Mr R.		5	0
Kenrick, Mrs T.	5	0	0	Walker & Kempson, Messrs.	10	0	0
Lees, Mr H.	5	0	0	Wykes, Mr T.A.		10	6
Matts, Mr		2	6	White, Mrs M.	1	1	0
Mott, Mr F.T.		10	6	Wardle, Mr P.A.		10	6
Norman, Mr H.		10	6	Wright, Mr M.	1	0	0
					102	13	0

Index

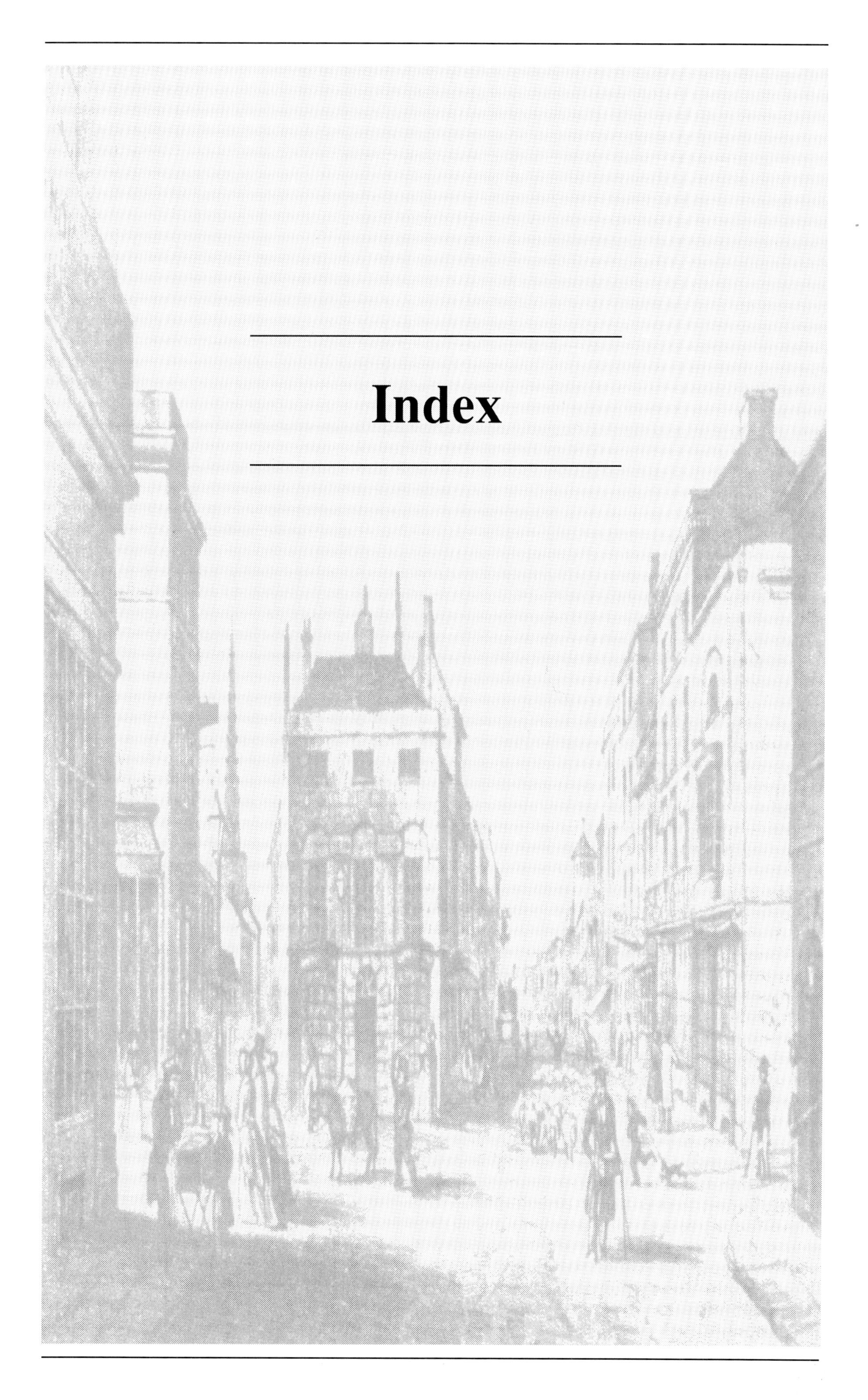

Horsefair Street c.1868

About the author

Barry Haynes, B.A., M. Phil., was born in Melton Mowbray, Leicestershire, and educated at Loughborough College School, Sheffield University, the London School of Economics and Leicester University. He is a specialist in nineteenth-century social history, his main interests being working-class history and class relationships. He has written a thesis and published articles in these areas. A schoolteacher for ten years, he is now a Research Associate at the Centre for Urban History, Leicester University and a lecturer in social history. He is married with two children and lives in Stoneygate, Leicester.